Single KNOW More

Single K**NO**W *More*

BUILD A HEALTHY FOUNDATION AND
ATTRACT THE LOVE YOU DESERVE

JOYCE NOVAK

NOVAK
PUBLISHING

Single KNOW More: Build a Healthy Foundation and Attract
the Love You Deserve
by Joyce Novak

Published by

Cover design by Lesia T.
Interior design by Nick Z, Journey Bound Publishing
Editing by Peggy Henrikson, Heart and Soul Editing

ISBN: 979-8-218-40825-1 (Paperback)
ISBN: 979-8-218-41032-2 (Ebook)

Printed in the United States of America

First Edition

*To women of all ages who want to develop
better habits, live a healthy life, and attract the
loving, long-lasting relationship they deserve.*

Acknowledgments

Thank you most of all to the love of my life, my husband Tod, for loving me unconditionally and continually helping me grow personally and professionally.

I'm also grateful for all my failed relationships for teaching me valuable lessons (the good, the bad, and the hard).

Contents

Introduction

Congratulations, my friend, on your desire to work on building a healthy foundation! The saying *The house doesn't crumble if the foundation is good* is also true of your life. A solid, healthy foundation will help you overcome life's challenges and distractions more quickly and confidently. Your life will be less stressful, and you won't crumble when events threaten to knock you down! Plus, you will be more likely to attract healthy relationships.

I learned this the hard way over time. I married my high school sweetheart, and a couple of years into the marriage it started falling apart. I knew at the time our marriage couldn't be repaired. After eight years of letting insecurity and fear control me, I finally got the courage to end the marriage.

My life completely changed. I was now living on my own, supporting myself, and navigating a lot of life situations alone. Ending my marriage was one of my scariest decisions ever. Looking back I wish I hadn't waited so many years, but I'm thankful I finally gained the courage to do it.

After being divorced for approximately nine months, I decided it was time to get out and start dating. Of course I had no idea it would take fifteen years to meet the man of my dreams.

During those dating years, I fully experienced single life and earned a lot of dating story badges—the good, the bad, and the ugly! All of my dating experiences and everything I learned during my single journey helped shape and build my foundation for the life I'm blessed to have today. I continue to get cracks in my foundation, but I've learned how to repair them quickly before they cause further damage.

My guess is when you look back at your life, you've said to yourself: *If only I'd have done that differently or would've known this, I might be in a better or different place right now. I wish I could go back in time and do it all over again.*

My advice is not to dwell on the past. Learn from it and keep moving forward, but don't live in the future, either. Yes, have goals and dreams, but live in the *present* each day and enjoy life, because we're not guaranteed tomorrow.

In each chapter of this book, I share personal experiences over the years to help you build a solid foundation and begin focusing on living your best healthy life right now and in the future. Not only do I share what I learned and experienced during my single journey, but what I'm currently working on and learning about life and love. I'm very proud of the life I've grown into and want to share my wisdom and experiences to help encourage you and others. Growing and learning never end; the process is a lifelong commitment.

If I can inspire you to feel more confident, build better habits, realize your self-worth, or help save you heartbreak and find love, this book will have served its purpose!

Chapter 1

LOVING and RESPECTING YOURSELF

Eat like you love yourself.
Move like you love yourself.
Speak like you love yourself.
Act like you love yourself.
Love yourself.
~ Anonymous

A healthy foundation starts with loving and respecting *yourself!* Having a healthy relationship with yourself is the first step to positive, balanced relationships in all areas of your life. Too many people are looking for the *right* person or *right* relationship instead of starting with themselves and getting their own life right.

Before you bring someone else into your life, you need to love and respect yourself! Respecting yourself will motivate you to make healthy choices in all areas of your life. Then, when you're the best version of yourself and feeling confident, you'll attract others who are healthy and confident.

Here's the key: The way you treat *yourself* sets the standard for how you want others to treat you.

If you *don't* think you're smart,

if you *don't* think you're pretty,

if you *don't* think you deserve more,

then guess what?

Nobody else will either.

You will attract what you believe you are worth.

As easy as it might sound, loving and respecting yourself can be difficult, because it includes accepting and embracing imperfections. *We. All. Have. Imperfections.* Some imperfections can be changed or improved and some can't. Once you realize it's okay to have imperfections and embrace them, you will attract people who respect you and all you have to offer, including your imperfections.

You are the driver of your life, so don't put the steering wheel in other people's hands. You are meant to direct your life; it's your story, your personal journey. Nobody knows you better than you!

Something I continually work on is perfectionism. It seems no matter what I do, I'm tempted to feel it's never quite good enough; so I end up spending way too much time working on projects or thinking about how I can make things better. However, I've learned over the years not to get stuck in perfectionism, because it sucks up my time, makes me feel not good enough, and holds me back. Living a healthy, productive life with imperfections is much more satisfying than attempting to live a "perfect" life! How draining that can be.

Love Yourself Inside and Out

Some of us seem to easily love others and give a lot, but when it comes to loving ourselves, we have a difficult time of it. We may think giving to others will add to our worth. Sadly, our giving might end up wearing us out if we don't balance it by taking care of ourselves. Many of us don't realize our worth is inherent and we don't have to earn it.

Self-acceptance comes from within, and this is why it's important to work on inner feelings and thoughts. We are happy and fulfilled mostly by who we are on the inside, and our internal lives contribute to producing our external circumstances.

When you see someone who looks gorgeous and all put together (beautiful hair, flawless skin, perfect makeup, stunning outfit, great body), you probably think, *WOW! She has it all together and must have an awesome life.* You can see a lot of this on social media, but I know, and I hope you know, most of the time what you see on social media is not reality. Photo filters are available that make people look perfect, for one thing. Plus, how people portray their lives on social media could be a lot of BS and not represent their *real* life.

I admit, I've felt down or inadequate after seeing people on social media who appear to be living extravagant and what seem to be perfect lives. But I also know most of what I'm seeing is not the way it really is.

I'm all for the occasional photo filter, but gals, using filters for every social media post is deceiving, especially when dating.

A filter can take several years off a person's actual age, make their eyes appear bigger, skin smooth and flawless, lips fuller, teeth whiter, and lashes longer. When someone posts a filtered photo, they may receive comments such as *You're so beautiful... You never age.... Gorgeous!* I'm sure those comments feel great and the person posting wants to continue receiving flattering comments so she continues to post filtered photos.

When someone continually posts filtered photos on social media, I intentionally don't comment or "like" them.

When you see a beautiful, well-put-together woman, you might think it's easy for her to have self-love, find the man of her dreams, feel confident, have an awesome career, and live a wonderful, happy life. But what you can't see is how she feels on the inside, which could present a totally different picture. Her thoughts and beliefs might be holding her back from what she deeply wants and desires in life. She may

Single KNOW More

have trouble dating guys who treat her with love and respect, having a close, loving bond with her family, going after her goals and dreams, or facing her fears. On the inside, she may not feel beautiful. She may feel lonely and unworthy. We just *assume* the opposite because she looks perfect.

When I've seen a female who's super fit, I've thought to myself, *If my body looked like that, I would feel more confident. I could wear any outfit and look great.*

On the flipside, the fit woman might see photos of me and my husband and think her life would be more complete and satisfying if she had a loving relationship with someone who loved her unconditionally.

I think at times we all have a little envy, but those thoughts should be fuel for us to strive to achieve whatever we envy. We don't want to be a hater or let someone's success get us down. Rather, we can use it as a motivator to better ourselves. Being happy for others for their success signals that's what we want for ourselves and makes it more likely we'll manifest it.

The truth is, if we all put consistent intention and effort into what we want, we could achieve our goals. It takes dedication and a strong mindset, and that's why a lot of people fail to get what they desire.

I also know that when I see people who are in great shape, more than likely they have a healthy diet and work out consistently, with the discipline to achieve that fitness, and I admire them and their effort. Professional athletes are a great example of the years of disciplined effort and determined mindset it takes to reach goals and be the best.

The most sabotaging force that can keep you from achieving your goals and your happiness is your very own mind. Negative thoughts can generate feelings that are incompatible with your positive goals. Fortunately, you can take control of your mind.

Dealing with Your Thoughts and Feelings

Do you need to connect with your inner self? Do you have inner chaos you need to acknowledge and heal? Your inner self, or mind, usually dictates what you do and how you feel. That said, it's normal to get discouraged or sad at times.

- You might go through a breakup and feel depressed.

- A loved one may pass away, and you grieve.

- You may blow your diet and feel frustrated and discouraged.

It's okay and human to feel negative emotions—but you don't want to stay stuck in them. Keeping your mind disciplined is part of good mental health. Then you can bounce back from sad or stressful times in your life. Also, with good mental health, you have the ability to express and manage emotions during change and uncertainty.

The key is to learn how to keep such feelings from knocking you off course. Sadness is a feeling you feel and move through, but it isn't meant to last a long time. Left unchecked, it will consume you. It can get out of control and turn into depression.

When you find yourself getting stuck in sadness, tackle it. Only *you* can control how you feel. You can't heal what you stuff and hide inside.

Following are a few healthy ways to deal with sadness.

1. **Keep going; keep your body moving.** Don't lie in bed all day or lounge on the sofa watching TV and eating junk food. Get outside and enjoy nature. Go for a walk. Go to the gym or yoga studio. Exercising increases serotonin, the feel-good hormone. It will help clear your mind and get you out of a funk. Exercise is a great anti-depressant and it's *free!*

2. **Conduct an internal audit.** What are you thinking about? What is making you feel sad? Ask yourself: *What am I doing in my life to create these feelings? Who am I hanging out with? Who am I idolizing? What am I watching on TV? Am I filling my head daily with negativity?*

   Experts say that if you cancel one negative thought with five positive ones, you can offset the typical negativity bias.[1] So constantly work on filling your mind with *positive* thoughts, and you'll eventually cancel out the negative ones.

3. **Do not depend on yourself.** Reach out to others. Meet a friend for coffee or lunch, or call a friend or family member and have a conversation. Talk it out. Don't just communicate by texting. We all need and

crave human connection and interaction. Talk to someone you know will listen to you and give you good advice. Don't call your Debbie Downer friend who may make you feel worse.

If you take a pill or drink alcohol to feel at peace or numb a problem, you may feel good for a little while, but you are temporarily masking the problem and damaging your body with the side effects of meds or alcohol. Too many people these days are on medication. Sometimes this simply delays or prevents resolution. The only way to sustain health and happiness permanently is to get to the root cause of what's triggering that unsettled, unpeaceful feeling so you can work on resolving it in a healthy manner.

We're more in tune with our *outer* self, because it's obviously easier to identify what we need to work on:

- ♥ If we need to lose a few pounds, we notice it on a daily basis when our jeans are a little snug or we can pinch more than an inch here and there.

- ♥ If our hair needs maintenance, we can see that the roots are dark or gray, or the ends are split. It's obvious we need to make an appointment with our hairdresser.

- ♥ If our skin is dry and flakey, we know it's time to exfoliate, moisturize, or use that hydrating mask that's been sitting in the drawer.

     Single KNOW More

Our inner self, however, is about thoughts and feelings, which we can't physically see. It's easier to hold them all in so we don't have to confront and work on them.

If we're not happy and confident with who we are, we may look to other people to make us feel good, and we may be attracting the wrong people into our life. Once we get our inner self right, it will reflect on the outside by how we live our life and the people we're attracting.

I know working on ourselves takes time and we're all busy. Most days we rush through the day juggling what needs to be accomplished. We go through our to-do list, and unexpected things come up, leaving no time in the rest of the day to work on ourselves. Or, we just don't have the energy to do it.

We all have work to do, whether it's on our outside or inside, and this work unfortunately never ends. It's called self-maintenance or self-love, and it requires continuous focus and effort. It's not selfish. We need to make time for it! We all deserve it!

Self-maintenance doesn't stop when we reach a certain age, but it can get more challenging as we get older. If we consistently work on improving and loving ourselves, however, our life can become more and more fulfilling.

The bottom line? Working on loving yourself is going to allow all other areas of your life to open up, bloom, and flourish.

A Friend Who Seemed to Have It All Together

When I was single and lived in Las Vegas, one of my girlfriends (fictitious name Brittany) was married. She had a perfect petite body, beautiful skin, and gorgeous blonde hair. Brittany and her husband owned a successful mortgage business, and they lived in a beautiful home.

Whenever I spent time with Brittany and her husband, they got along great and spoke to each other with respect. They seemed to be a happy couple.

When Brittany and I had one-on-one conversations, she didn't mention any marriage problems other than small things many of us gripe about in relationships. In my eyes, her life seemed awesome!

One day after we'd gone shopping together and she was driving up to the front of my house to drop me off, she said that she wanted to tell me something. I had no clue what she was going to say, so I was apprehensive.

She told me she was getting a divorce. *What?!* I was in complete shock. How did I not know she had serious issues with her marriage? Was I a bad friend because I didn't know what was going on? Should I have noticed hints or signs that things were going south even though she didn't verbally tell me?

This is the perfect example of how people hold in their troubles so friends or even family members, as close as we are to them, have no clue what they're going through. Some people can hide things quite effectively, while others are quick to share their feelings and life story. Obviously, my friend chose to keep her marriage issues bottled up. Even though I couldn't believe that Brittany didn't share with me what was really happening, it's normal to want to avoid exposing our vulnerabilities to others.

No one wants to be judged, so it's never a good idea to judge how others live their life or assume how they're feeling. Unless they tell you, you have no idea what they're going through on the inside and what struggles they're battling. They may look like they have it all together on the outside but feel broken on the inside and want to mask the hurt. Just because someone carries it well, doesn't mean it's not heavy.

This example of my friend is a good reminder not to be envious of what you perceive others have and to be thankful for everything *you* have, even if it's not much at the time. Gratitude attracts more good into your life.

Self-Care

To love yourself means to take care of yourself. We hear a lot about self-care these days. Most women when they hear that expression think of taking time to relax, soaking in a bubble bath, going on a vacation, or getting a massage, pedicure, or facial. Those are all great for self-care, and I love all of them. However, self-care sometimes involves doing something that's not so pleasant, or maybe even painful. We may tend to avoid things such as going to the dentist or working out and choose the bubble bath instead.

Exercising is especially important to me and to Tod as well. I put our exercise schedule on the calendar and try hard not to schedule anything else during that time so we can stay on track and get our workouts in. Of course, sometimes life and work obligations throw off the schedule, but we get back on track ASAP.

Many times I have to push through self-care activities. On workout days, I usually don't want to get out of bed early. I would prefer to sleep a little later or just dive into work. Some days, I prefer not to work out at all. I'm well aware, however, that sleeping in and not working out won't help me stay healthy and fit. I want to feel good, have energy, and keep my body in shape, so I push through the workouts and continually remind myself of the benefits! Most of the time, I exercise with my husband. As a bonus, we encourage each other through workouts, just as we continually encourage and motivate each other through life.

When I was single, if I didn't work out with a friend, I enjoyed group classes at the gym such as spin, strength training, and yoga. Being in a room full of other people exercising was motivating and helped me complete workouts. Some people enjoy working out alone, but I do better with the extra push I get from working out with others.

It's easy to get stuck in thinking about why you don't want to do something such as exercise, but change your focus to the benefits and the desired outcome you'll achieve. Don't focus on the negatives; focus on the positive results.

Daily Care Routines

Beneficial daily habits can help boost self-esteem. A lot of nights I'm tired and I would love to just fall into bed and go to sleep. But I know I have to do my nightly routine before putting my head on the pillow and closing my eyes. It goes something like this:

- ♥ Put my pj's on (I have a slight obsession with pj's and slippers).

- ♥ Waterpik, floss, and brush my teeth.

- ♥ Cleanse, tone, and moisturize my face and neck.

- ♥ Apply eye cream.

- ♥ Moisturize my hands.

This routine is a tiny sliver of my daily self-care and hygiene that pays off big time in the long run to keep me feeling good and my skin looking healthy. I recall only two times I didn't wash my face before going to bed; it's that important to me.

A little tip that works for me: A few hours before I go to bed, I put on my pj's and go through my nightly routine. That way, when my eyes get heavy and I feel tired, I can go directly to bed. Doing my nightly routine earlier in the evening works well for me, because when I do it right before bed, sometimes splashing water on my face and putting product on it wakes me up a little. Then I have a harder time falling asleep.

You will never regret daily routines and healthy habits. They're part of self-care and a healthy lifestyle. Developing daily routines can help you feel more in control of your day.

Healthy Eating

Self-care also involves eating healthy food to support your body. Some days I don't want to prepare meals. Cooking at home is time consuming, and it's challenging to come up with different meals to cook every day. Certain meals I cook often, but I also like to come up with new recipes to help keep our meals from getting boring. Lately I've acquired lots of great recipes using an Instant Pot and Air Fryer, which has helped add variety to our meals.

Of course cooking at home involves more than coming up with meal ideas. I have to shop for the ingredients, prep, cook, then clean up the kitchen. It takes time, energy, and effort. It's much easier to order something in or go to a restaurant and be served—but those options aren't as healthy as cooking at home. Often, food tastes yummy at restaurants because, more than likely, it contains a lot of salt, butter, and fattening ingredients. Those ingredients, my friend, may make everything taste better, but they certainly aren't healthy. Tod and I can always tell when meals at restaurants are prepared with healthy ingredients because our stomachs aren't bloated and hurting after the meal. Because we eat healthy food most of the time, our stomachs are sensitive and on point. They "know."

Healthy home cooking can have a huge impact on our overall health, so I consider this a big part of my self-care. I'm not willing to give up eating healthy meals just for convenience, so I normally take the time and effort to prepare meals at home.

The food you eat plays a big part in how you feel, your weight, and how much energy you have. Food is *brain medicine,* and the good part is you can control what you eat. If you're eating a lot of sugar-laden and fatty foods, you're probably feeling tired and sluggish a lot of the time and gaining a few pounds. Start your day right with a healthy breakfast and set the tone for the day.

Of course Tod and I have cheat days, but the *key* is to stick with a healthy routine, and we strive for that. If we get off track, we get back on track ASAP. Bouncing back from eating unhealthy food for a few days is much easier than after eating it for a week.

Daily Journal/Blessing Book

The quality of your life reflects what you do *consistently,* not just sometimes when you feel like it. Almost everything you do in life is the result of your habits, and your daily habits decide your future. If you establish good habits, you will excel and achieve goals. If you fall into bad habits, you will continually be disappointed and make no progress. A good way to stay on track is by keeping a daily journal of your activities and meals. You can use the same journal to jot down a few things each day for which you're grateful.

Tod and I have a Blessing Book, and together we jot down blessings as they happen in our life. This book is such a joy to look through as a reminder of how blessed we are and to continue to stay grateful. It's an extra joy looking through our entries and reflecting when we're having a not-so-good day or a tough season. It's a great reminder of all we have to be thankful for.

Some days I have so many items on my to-do list, it can be overwhelming, and that's when stress can creep in and make me a little edgy. To help keep me from feeling overwhelmed, I tackle the most important things on my to-do list and know I have tomorrow to complete other tasks I didn't get to.

My husband and I have a good balance with the negative/positive. When something negative happens, sometimes I tend to get a bit stuck in it. I'm getting better at controlling this, but it's work in progress. On the other hand, my husband is one of the most positive people I know. If something negative happens, he quickly flips it to a positive.

The good thing is you don't have to have a husband to do this! You can do it on your own, if you create a habit of it. The more positive you are, the better chance you have of attracting positive relationships and circumstances in your life.

A good way to keep peace in your life is to fill your mind and spirit with positive thoughts and surround yourself with uplifting, positive people. You are responsible for your thoughts, feelings, and actions. You can't stop occasional negative thoughts from entering your mind, but you can control them once they get there and determine how long you engage with them. You are in charge: Don't let negative thoughts take control!

Have you ever noticed when you spend time with positive people, you feel positive? I know when I have a lot of energy and feel good and productive, Tod also has the same vibe. It's almost as if it rubs off on him. And vice versa: When one of us is in a negative mood, it seems to set the tone.

Of course we can't always be in a positive, upbeat mood because we're human and have multiple feelings. The key is knowing how and when to flip the switch.

Accepting Compliments

When you love yourself and have confidence, you can accept and embrace compliments. You are worthy of compliments—acknowledge them!

It took me a long time to feel comfortable accepting compliments. I used to talk them down. For example, if someone said, "I love your shirt," I would say something like, "I've had it forever," or "It's comfortable," or "I got a great deal on it." I couldn't just say "Thank you." Now, I don't second guess a compliment; I receive it with a smile and gratitude.

One day when I was at a hair appointment, the sun was shining brightly through the window near where I was sitting. As you probably have experienced, natural sunlight on skin shows every imperfection. As I was sitting in the chair waiting for my hairdresser to mix up the color for my hair, I looked in the mirror at myself and the natural light was unforgiving. At that moment I didn't feel attractive because every flaw was magnified. Despite my feeling, at the end of my appointment my hairdresser commented, "You look so pretty, you remind me of a movie star. You've just got that look." Perfect timing for a compliment! It definitely gave me a boost and changed my mindset.

When was the last time you complimented someone? People love compliments, and it could make someone's day. I'm talking about true compliments, not phony compliments just to make conversation or kiss up to someone. Be authentic and mean it when you give a compliment.

Today, I challenge you to genuinely compliment someone and notice how it makes them feel. I bet it will bring a smile not only to their face but to your face as well. Nobody is ever going to be offended if you compliment them.

Aging and Loving Yourself

Loving yourself may get a little more challenging as you age. I know firsthand it can be challenging to accept and embrace the changes that come along with aging. Skin loses elasticity, gray hair appears, extra pounds creep on, and energy levels decrease.

My advice? If you're in your twenties, *now* is the time to invest in a healthy lifestyle, if you haven't already. Trust me, as you advance in age, you'll be thankful you did. You have only one body, and it has to last a lifetime, so you can never be too young or too old to be kind to your body and invest in it.

Never let your age limit your self-care *or* keep you from starting a new chapter in your life. Some women find aging so stressful they feel as if they have to lie about their age when dating. I can relate, but I didn't lie about my age. I'm lucky that I've always looked younger than my actual age. I'm not bragging and certainly not complaining. I feel truly blessed for my great genes—but I've taken care of my body and health, and it's paid off as I age.

When I was in my late thirties and single, when a guy approached me to start a conversation, I knew he was probably thinking I was younger—maybe around thirty-two. It made me a little nervous, knowing age would eventually come up in conversation. A few years age difference may not sound like a big deal, but trust me, when you're a single woman and over the age of thirty-five, every year seems to count when dating. Why start off a relationship with a lie? If my age was going to be an issue, I wanted to know right away before investing my time and energy in the relationship.

I suggest if you're seriously looking for a long-term relationship, never lie about your age or use old photos on your dating profiles and social media. With so many filter options for photos available now, who knows how someone really looks? But the truth comes out eventually! Filters only work on photos—not in real life. You don't want a guy to be totally shocked when he meets you in person after seeing only filtered photos of you.

I personally know a few people who don't look like their filtered photos on social media. I don't use filters, but I'm not saying I will never use filters. I might use them once in a while for fun, but using them on a daily basis is deceiving and a bit cheesy, in my opinion. I guess that's part of the social media world we live in now—a lot of deception.

With the internet at our fingertips, it's easy to find out a lot of information about someone, including age. So save yourself the embarrassment of getting caught in a lie. Don't lie about your age, as tempting as it might be. The best advice I have is to embrace your age and continually work on staying healthy and fit.

Ladies, you might be forty and attracted to twenty-five-year-old men. Unless you're just looking for the occasional fun date, you need to think about the future. Think about what your relationship might be like down the road when you are fifty (starting to go through menopause) and he is thirty-five in his prime and decides out of the blue he wants a baby. Or he wants to party every weekend and the party scene is no longer appealing to you. Those are just a couple of the many issues that could arise with a large age gap. Aging is difficult enough in itself, but when you're with a man who's a lot younger than you, it can become more and more stressful the older you get.

I highly recommend dating and marrying a partner close to your age. It will make for a more comfortable and lasting relationship as you get older and experience life together. Not everyone will agree with this, but I'm speaking from my own experience. I dated both younger and older men. My husband is one year older than I am, and it works great for us.

I believe you can find love at any age, so don't use the excuse that you're too old or it's too late. There's no age limit for love or success. I've personally witnessed women and men in their sixties and beyond finding love. After my beautiful mom passed away, my dad found love again when he was in his sixties.

When I was thirty-seven, I felt old. I know, this sounds absolutely crazy, but a breakup triggered my feeling old at thirty-seven. I was in a one-and-a-half-year relationship I thought would be "the one"—until it wasn't. This breakup was especially difficult for me, and it was even more emotionally painful because I started feeling the aging vibe.

In the midst of the breakup, my ex and I exchanged a few hasty words, and during that heated conversation, he said, "I will find someone younger." I was surprised to hear him say this because he was just two years younger than I was.

Those five words drove a sword deep into my heart, which stuck there. I kept hearing those words in my head, and because I focused on those hurtful words, I started believing I was old at age thirty-seven—too old to find love. I think those harsh words hit me with even more force because, at that age, my biological clock was ticking. But would it still be ticking by the time I found love again and got married? I definitely felt the pressure.

Thank goodness it didn't take long for me to realize feeling old at thirty-seven was a crazy and insecure thought. Plus, as it turned out, this breakup was actually a blessing. Of course I didn't realize it at the time, but looking back, I can see the flaws in that relationship, and I'm thankful it didn't work out.

Keep in mind that if you're rejected, it may well mean you're being redirected to something better.

What he said to me is a perfect example of how words can carry tremendous weight. Before you blurt out ugly words in a heated moment that may hurt someone, take a few seconds and think about what is about to come out of your mouth and the lasting impact your words might have on someone. You can apologize, but you can't take words back once you put them out there. This also applies to social media. Social media has made it easier to blurt out mean comments. People are brave hiding behind a screen and saying comments they would never say to someone face to face.

> *"The tongue is a small thing, but what enormous*
> *damage it can do."*
> ~ James 3:5-6, TLB

When you learn to love yourself, you have begun the journey of becoming genuinely happy.

The next chapter addresses change and the different "seasons" we go through in our lives, in particular, our "single season" with its ups and downs. Loving yourself can provide the strong roots you need to weather any storm.

EMBRACING YOUR SINGLE "SEASON"

Appreciate being single because
that's when you grow the most . . .
and with that growth, you come
to know what you're looking for.
~ Daniel Goddard

Life continually changes, just like the four seasons of spring, summer, fall, and winter. Fall is my favorite season. The air is crisp and an abundance of pumpkin is everywhere. Fall is the homestretch of finishing out the year, heading into the holiday season.

I have memories of fall when I was a young girl and lived in Iowa. We had several huge trees in our yard. I always looked forward to when my dad would rake the leaves into a huge pile and my brothers and sisters and I would jump into it. That was such a fun thing to do in the fall as a child.

In many parts of the country, fall brings the beauty of vibrantly colored trees with leaves of orange, yellow, gold, and red. Then the leaves turn brown and fall from the branches, and all of sudden the trees are no longer colorful and beautiful, but bare. The crispy brown leaves blow away in the wind or get raked up and are gone. The barren trees go dormant and embrace the change in season, which is usually harsher with cooler temperatures. Depending on where in the country the trees are growing, it can be snowy with freezing temperatures.

Every year, the trees survive this harsh season until spring rolls around and they burst out with bright green buds or gorgeous blooms.

Developing Strong Roots

How do the trees survive the severity of winter? They survive because they have strong roots.

Just like trees, we continually go through seasons, although the timing of our seasons isn't so regular. Some of our seasons are vibrant and beautiful and some are harsh and cold. Just

Single KNOW More

like the trees, it's much easier for us to make it through harsh seasons if we have *strong roots—a solid foundation.*

Relationships go through many seasons, and you need a strong foundation to weather them. It doesn't matter if you're single or married or how old you are, like all of us, you will go through many different seasons throughout life. Learning to navigate the changing seasons helps you grow. The great thing is that, unlike a tree, for the most part you have the power to control your seasons and the length of time you choose to stay in each one.

Some of you may currently be in a vibrant, cheerful, beautiful season, and I'm sure it feels awesome. Some of you are in a dark season of heartbreak, career challenges, financial issues, or just trying to get by.

It's hard to imagine when you're struggling through a dark season that a brighter season is ahead. But sometimes you need to experience dark seasons to get to where you want to be.

I went through years of breakups and heartbreaks and jobs I didn't like, and I have lived in four different states. All of my experiences helped shape where I am today. In the midst of my dark seasons, I didn't see the brighter season, the better future, ahead of me. As much as I love my current life, I still experience challenging seasons and always will. Now, however, I'm better equipped to take them on and kick their butt!

When you hit a harsh season, you need to keep going and fight through it; otherwise, it will linger and fester. Consider these strategies:

- ♥ First of all, acknowledge what's going on in your life and determine how you got to this point.

- ♥ Don't mope around for weeks or months and feel sorry for yourself. I know that's a lot easier said than done, but you need to keep moving forward!

- ♥ Don't blame others, even though they may have played a part in your dark season. It's not up to them to make your life happy. Take responsibility and start working on a solution.

- ♥ Fill your mind and spirit with positivity. Read uplifting books, listen to motivating podcasts, and surround yourself with upbeat people.

- ♥ Tell yourself over and over again, *"I can do this! I am smart, I'm a fighter, I'm not going to give up, and I deserve to live a great life!"*

- ♥ Block negativity from your life, which may include not watching the news, limiting your time on social media, and avoiding toxic people.

When you're in a dark place and you feel like you've been buried deep in the dirt, think of it this way: Maybe you've actually been planted and need some time to sprout and grow. Trust in the process and do everything you can to move forward.

Dark seasons can be stormy and disrupt your life, but if you persevere through the storms, it will lead you to brighter skies and sunny days!

Single KNOW More

If you're in a happy season, *enjoy* it, live in the moment, open your heart, and take it all in. Be thankful. Bless others with your cheer.

Seasons are also a time of growth, so be open to learn from them. Seasons—good and bad—are what we need for *transformation.*

Learn from bad experiences so they won't keep repeating, and don't take happy ones for granted. Learn how you can duplicate your successes and great feelings.

When I look back at my life, I'm thankful for almost all of my seasons (good, bad, and ugly), because all my seasons taught me valuable life lessons. They stretched me and made me the happy woman I am today.

God intentionally created us to grow, change, and learn over time, and this growth happens through different seasons, which never end. The season we're currently in could be preparing us for what's next in our life, and the exciting thing is, we never know what's next! But we can be sure that our outcomes will depend on our focus and actions.

Dealing with Change

My personality type sometimes resists change because change means moving into something different and unknown. I typically like things familiar and safe, but I also know and have learned over the years that if I'm not changing, I'm not growing.

Growth is our greatest superpower! What we focus on grows, so we need to focus on improving every area of our lives. When we change in positive ways—become happier and better able to meet the challenges of life—we feel *alive*. It's healthy to grow.

Experience new opportunities, stretch yourself, face your fears. Anyone who really loves you won't try to hold you back or discourage you from growing and changing. They will *support* your growth and be *happy* for your successes. Your partner should always have your back.

Tod and I have each other's back and we know we can count on each other, but this didn't happen overnight. It took years of trust and knowing how the other person thinks and feels.

Change and growth are difficult, but they make us stronger. We naturally don't want to do difficult things, so we resist. However, staying in our comfort zone throughout life can actually make us weak, lazy, and unmotivated.

Remember: Whatever you are *not changing* you are *choosing* to have in your life!

I'll give you a great example of someone resisting change and not wanting to grow, even though she complained about her current circumstances.

My husband and I were working with a client's staff member who made a comment that surprised us. She said she didn't need personal development because she had learned everything about that already. She felt she knew all she needed to know.

Really? She'd learned *everything* there is to know about growing personally and professionally? Isn't part of learning and growing keeping up with current material and stretching

   Single K**NO**W More

yourself? *Personal Development Tip:* Learning doesn't have an expiration date; it should be happening every day!

This was a lady who complained about 75 percent of the time and was highly negative. I'm not sure what personal development material she'd read or studied, but it clearly hadn't helped her. Most of the time, personal growth is tough because it's challenging to admit one's flaws and work on them. Apparently she didn't want to admit she had any flaws because she didn't want to work on them.

Although she didn't want to take personal responsibility for it, during her coaching sessions with Tod the woman did express a problem. She said she wasn't making enough money to cover her bills and was struggling financially. Tod, as he does with his clients, went to bat for her. He helped her get a raise and a bonus so she wouldn't have the burden of worrying about not being able to pay her bills. She could then feel more at ease and less stressed, which in turn would help her work performance.

Of course Tod analyzed her position and her responsibilities to justify the increase in pay, and she had not received a pay increase in several years. To be clear, the raise and bonus weren't just given to her because she complained and couldn't pay her bills; they were justified. *But,* she wouldn't have received them if Tod hadn't intervened and gone to bat for her.

You're probably thinking she was really grateful and thanked Tod for his help, that maybe she gave him a thank you card or sent him an email thanking him or gave him a call to show her appreciation. No, just the opposite. Instead of a thank you, within a week she stabbed him in the back. What kind of person does that? I'll tell you: someone who has deep issues. She said she knew everything there is to know about personal development, but she was in denial. She refused to work on her inner issues, refused to be grateful, and refused to be happy. Tod helped remove a huge burden for her, but she still just wanted to complain and hurt others.

The moral of this story is that everyone needs to be healing as needed, growing, and learning every single day. Whether we believe it or not, we need to work on personal development our entire life. We should never think we know it all.

One of my husband's favorite old sayings is, *"Either you are green and growing or ripe and rotting."*

Taking Advantage of Your Single Season

Your "single season" is a good time to not only work on your self-development but to build strong bonds with friends. When you're in a relationship, your partner will probably take up most of your free time. But don't diss friends altogether once you find a partner. Friendships are healthy and needed.

Besides spending time with friends, I also spent a lot of my free time exercising. I went to the gym almost every night after work and at least once over the weekend. The gym was filled with people and energy, and that was much better than going home to an empty place after work. As a bonus, I was in fantastic shape.

I suggest you take advantage of those pockets of time when you may not want to be alone to hit the gym, or perhaps get outside, breathe in fresh air, and enjoy nature. Admire the beautiful trees and flowers; watch wildlife. Take a walk or a bike ride. Doing activities and finding ways to move your body will keep you busy in a beneficial way and keep your creative juices flowing. It will get you out of the house, you will have more energy and feel more motivated, and it will help keep you in shape and healthy. You can never go wrong with moving your body and being active! *Don't get in the habit of being lazy. It can be a hard habit to break* and a lot of other villains can sneak in, such as weight gain and depression.

When you're single and your friends and family are busy with their lives, it's okay to go to dinner or a movie by yourself, or go to a coffee shop. Not everyone is comfortable and feels confident doing this alone, and I understand because it was hard for me to do certain things solo.

However, it's good to get out and be around other people. When you go out by yourself, don't just sit and bury your face in your laptop or cell phone; have conversations when you get the chance; smile and make eye contact with people. It will help you to not feel alone, and you just might meet a new friend or maybe your dream guy!

Someone gave me a bit of advice that stayed in my mind: "Enjoy being single, Joyce, because you could meet the man of your dreams tomorrow and your life will change. Just like that, you will not be single anymore. Enjoy all that being single has to offer."

That advice brought to light how quickly my single season could change. It helped me become more mindful of taking full advantage of that time, soaking it all in and enjoying it.

Your single season is a great time for you to work on yourself and enjoy many activities and people you won't have as much time for once you find a partner.

Managing Difficult Times During Single Season

For me, one of the most difficult times being single was during the holidays. A lot of emotions naturally come up over the holidays. Plus, of course, some weekends were lonely living alone. I would much rather wake up on a lazy Saturday or Sunday morning and have coffee with a significant other than by myself.

Most of my single life I didn't have family living near me, so if I didn't travel to see my family for holidays or spend holidays with friends, I was alone. I was most fortunate in that I only had to be alone for holidays a handful of times.

Christmas was my least favorite holiday to spend alone, but one Christmas I was able to put that time to good use. I was working then as a licensed esthetician in Newport Beach, California. I love beauty treatments and beauty products, and a beauty treatment I like that has good results is a medical-grade facial peel. With that kind of peel, the top layer of skin on your face literally peels off, revealing a soft, fresh new layer of skin.

Although I love the outcome of peels, I don't love the downtime when my face looks scary! Thus, I rarely get them

 Single KNOW More

because the whole skin-peeling process of a good medical-grade chemical peel takes about a week.

Soooo, during that particular Christmas holiday I spent alone, my gift to myself was beautiful new skin on my face from a chemical peel.

My Christmas dinner that year consisted of a microwave Lean Cuisine pizza along with some microwave popcorn and champagne. How sad is that?! I didn't even cook a somewhat healthy meal. (FYI, I no longer eat frozen/microwave foods—not even the ones that claim to be healthy—because they're processed. And I *rarely* cook anything in the microwave.)

As I snuggled on the sofa Christmas Eve with skin peeling off my face, I watched a few movies on Lifetime. I loved watching chick flicks on Lifetime or *Sex and the City* reruns. It wasn't my ideal Christmas, for sure, but I made it through being alone, even on Christmas day.

The day after Christmas, it was time to get ready for a *new year*. Who doesn't love ringing in the new year? New dreams . . . new goals . . . maybe a new boyfriend . . .

The revelation of my Christmas Alone story is: I didn't let being alone get me down. Yeah, of course I felt a little sorry for myself being alone on Christmas, but I didn't get totally depressed. I had the right mindset and made the best of it because I knew I wouldn't be alone every single Christmas, which got me thinking: *I wonder where my life will be during the holidays next year.* And that was exciting because you never know what the future holds, and I knew I would be in a different season. So much can change in a year—or even in a month, a week, a day. Shift your mindset—shift your life.

Now I get to spend every Christmas with my husband, making wonderful memories together. So yes, I would do it all again (spending some holidays alone).

Encouraging Transformation

Whatever season you're in, push forward and live your best life *now!* Do things that you enjoy and live in the moment. Don't always be in a hurry; slow down and enjoy life because it goes by way too fast! Being in a hurry can make you miss the truly important things in life. Plus, if you don't take time for self-reflection, you won't know what or how to change for the better.

I was reminded of transformation on one of the runs that Tod and I took on a trail behind our house in California. It's a challenging run because the trail goes up a steep incline. It's worth the effort, though, because the scenery is so beautiful and peaceful. We've seen deer, rabbits, roadrunners, quail, and coyotes. When we get to the peak of the hill, we're rewarded with a view of the majestic Pacific Ocean.

One bright spring day when I was running, I noticed a lot of caterpillars inching their way along the trail. This made me think of the caterpillars' different seasons, or stages, of life. Caterpillars aren't very attractive, they move at a glacial pace, and they can't see anything except the ground upon which they crawl. Then, they cocoon themselves, hidden away in the dark. Eventually, they emerge into their new season as a butterfly—delicately beautiful, colorful, and able to flutter freely in the air, high above the ground. What a transformation of season from caterpillar to butterfly!

*"Just when the caterpillar thought her life was over,
she began to fly."*
~ Anonymous

During your single season, take advantage of all you can do to transform yourself into who you want to be. In addition, if you transform while you're single, you'll more likely attract a more transformed partner. Butterflies attract other butterflies, not caterpillars.

If you're lucky, as I was, you'll attract a partner who fully supports your *continuing* transformation. (In fact, put that on your list of what you want in a partner.)

For my birthday one year, my husband bought me a guitar. Why? Well, we'd been talking over dinner, and I told him I had played the guitar in Catholic grade school at church service every morning before school. I mentioned I hadn't played the guitar since then and that someday I'd like to take brush-up lessons and start playing again. It was just a random idea I threw out there over dinner. What did my thoughtful husband do? He bought me a guitar with an amplifier!

One of the many great qualities of my husband is he truly *listens* to me. This is wonderful—*and* I've learned to be careful what I wish for or say, because Tod *hears* me, and I usually get what I ask for. So then guitar lessons were in order!

Speaking of playing the guitar, who out there loves music?! Music is great food for the soul, *if* you're listening to the right music. It's amazing how a good song can get me going and make me feel happy or bring back memories. Some nights when I was single, home alone enjoying a glass of wine and a bag of microwave popcorn, I'd turn up the music and dance around my living room and sing. The best part was I could bust out my best moves and not have to worry about looking ridiculous. It felt so good!

Music can be powerful and beneficial. It can help relax you, lift your mood, reduce stress, and decrease blood pressure.[2]

Looking back at when I was listening to music a lot during the '80s and '90s, I wish I'd been more aware of the words in those songs. Honestly, I didn't think twice about the lyrics. When I met my husband, he pointed out some of the negative words in the songs I was listening to and singing so loudly with passion.

You might be thinking, Joyce, what's the big deal about listening to songs with a few negative lyrics or curse words? Well, whatever we hear (especially if we're singing) *enters our mind and affects our mood and actions.* That's reason enough for me to want to listen to positive *everything.*

I'm now fully aware that the way I think is controlled by what I'm putting or *letting* into my mind. I'm very careful about what I feed my mind, including what I watch on TV, how much news I watch, and what music I listen to.

My husband listens to a variety of music, including Christian music. I had never listened to Christian music (outside of church services) before I met Tod. I'm ashamed to say it kind of annoyed me when we first started dating that he listened to Christian music in the car or at home. But my

Single K**NO**W More

annoyance didn't stop him from listening to it, and I'm so glad it didn't, because now *I* love listening to Christian music as well. The words are uplifting and positive, and that's what I want to feed my mind and spirit.

I challenge you, the next time you listen to music, to pay attention to the words in the songs and ask yourself, *Is this what I want to feed my mind, which controls my thoughts and actions?*

For example, a song with a great beat that you probably shouldn't listen to frequently is called "I'm Bad at Love." The words "I'm bad at love" are continually repeated throughout the song. If you listen to it a lot, you may start feeling like you're . . . well . . . bad at love. I like to play a little game with songs that have negative lyrics: I reverse the lyrics and, for instance, sing, "I'm *good* at love." Those are words I'd prefer to have programmed into my mind!

Seasons aren't constantly shifting only in our lives; change is continuously happening everywhere around us.

Think about how music has changed throughout the years: '60s–'70s–'80s–'90s music.

Food is always changing: Twenty years ago, kale was placed around salad bars as decoration, and today kale is a popular healthy superfood that we eat in our salads and drink in our smoothies.

Technology has changed tremendously over the past decade—and it has changed the way we communicate and *date.*

What hasn't changed? L-O-V-E—LOVE
We *need* connection.
We *need* community.
We *need* LOVE.

Whatever you desire (your dream guy, dream job, dream home . . .), keep nourishing your mind with positive, healthy input. Be wise and discerning about what you take in and believe, for it all determines your life. *Visualize* that you already have what you want, *feel* that you deserve it, and you will attract what you want—*whatever* "season" you're in.

> *"Keep your heart with all vigilance,*
> *for from it flow the springs of life."*
> ~ Proverbs 4:23, ESV

Speaking of being vigilant, in the next chapter, we'll look at red and green flags in relationships. Lack of vigilance on your part can bring heartbreak—and vigilance can save you.

Chapter 3

RED FLAGS AND GREEN FLAGS IN A RELATIONSHIP

As we gain confidence in ourselves,
red flags are no longer red flags.
They are deal breakers.
~ Anonymous

’m beginning this chapter with one of my favorite sayings (source unknown): *When people show you their red flags, show them your white flag and peace out.*

Yes, leave peacefully and save yourself a lot of time and heartache.

Have you ever been in a relationship and something just didn't seem right or you didn't like a certain behavior of the other person that happened frequently? These uncomfortable feelings on your part in reaction to occurrences or behaviors of the other person are "red flags" for you. They indicate you need to reevaluate the relationship and either resolve the issue or dissolve the relationship.

All relationships involve red flags. I believe everyone who's been in any type of relationship, whether it's dating or a relationship with a friend, family member, or co-worker, has experienced red flags.

As it would be impossible for me to cover every possible red flag, I'll cover seven that are at the top of my list. I'll also share positive green flags to help you evaluate the potential of a relationship.

Seven Dating Red Flags You Shouldn't Ignore

When you sense a red flag in a relationship, are you the type of person who investigates and wants to get to the bottom of it? Or do you ignore red flags because it's easier and you're afraid they're related to something painful you may not want to know? Do you carry on because it's easier to deny that

                                    Single K**NO**W More

anything's wrong than to go through the potential pain or heartbreak of discovering there *is?*

Me? I'm a *digger!* Sometimes I think I should have been a private investigator because I think I'm pretty good at solving issues that need answers.

If you aren't investigating red flags, chances are you're in denial or fear. As painful as it might be, you always need to follow your gut instinct, or intuition, and get to the bottom of a suspicious situation.

To spot red flags, you need to be *aware.* Keep your eyes open and please don't just put your head in the sand like an ostrich. Be alert and in control of your life. Even if you think, *Oh, this is just a small red flag . . . no big deal,* over time, that small red flag could turn into a large red flag if you don't address it. Nip *all* red flags—small, medium and large—in the bud! Don't disregard them!

Red Flag #1: Physical Abuse

Fortunately, I have not experienced physical abuse in any of my relationships, and I attribute it to not attracting that type of man. I'm not saying I'm a better person or smarter because I didn't attract an abusive man. I believe my foundation of self-confidence, self-worth, and positive mindset played a big part in the type of men I attracted into my life.

If you're attracting abusive men repeatedly, it's time to figure out *why* this is happening so you can stop that pattern. Typically, when something happens repeatedly there's a common denominator. In this situation, that's more than likely *you.* Step back and figure out why this is happening. What's going on in your mind? What vibes are you radiating? Has something happened previously in your life that may have set you up to expect this? Our expectations, even if they're subconscious, can produce powerful attracting vibes.

You can change these patterns by consciously changing your expectations and choices. You need to become super sensitive to red flags and choose to avoid those people!

A tip that might be helpful: Journal about your relationships. Daily, write down your thoughts about your current relationship(s). What specific issues or problems arise and what provoked them? Were they resolved or did you brush them aside? Writing out your feelings and thoughts can bring issues to the surface you may not have been aware of. What your writing reveals may also help you determine areas to work on that will help you attract a different kind of man. Start refusing to accept any kind of abuse. It may be attention, but it's not the kind you want. It's not love!

The following statistic is alarming: *About one in four women will experience physical violence by an intimate partner in their lifetime.*[3] That's a 25 percent chance, which is huge! Please be aware and act on any type of physical abuse quickly. Respect yourself enough to not stay in an abusive relationship!

The first step to finding a healthy relationship is getting out of an unhealthy relationship.

Red Flag #2: Drug or Alcohol Abuse

Unfortunately a lot of activities and situations in our society involve drinking some form of alcohol. People pop champagne to celebrate; they make themselves a stiff drink to "relax" after a long day; they grab a drink when stress overwhelms them; and they drink alcohol to gain a little liquid courage.

When we see drinking in a TV show or movie, it may look sexy or cool. However, that doesn't mean you have to follow suit and drink five shots because the beautiful, cool chick in the movie did it. This, my friends, is not real life, and you will not feel glamorous the next morning when you wake up feeling miserable with a pounding headache.

If you or a family member or friend has experienced the effects of alcohol or drug abuse, you know how harmful and addictive it can be. If you're dating someone who has to drink alcohol or use drugs on a regular basis to have a good time or feel good or just make it through the day, *this is definitely a red flag.* If someone can't have a good time without drinking or drugs, deeper issues are involved. This behavior will eventually bring you both down and could possibly lead to verbal or physical abuse. Like most of us, you have probably experienced how alcohol or drugs can bring out the ugliest behavior.

If you are always bailing someone out who has an addiction, that person is not learning and you are *not* doing the person any good. Being in this type of relationship long term could take you both down the road of codependency, which is a lifelong battle.

Don't always feel the need or pressure to add alcohol to the mix to have a good time, and be sensitive to others who don't drink.

If you drink alcohol on a date, I suggest keeping it to one drink or no drinks for the first several dates, for many reasons. You obviously want to keep your composure and you don't want to say or do something you may regret the next day when you have a clear mind. Most of the time, getting a little loose lipped from drinking doesn't leave a good impression.

Also, during the first several months of dating, you're getting to know someone. You don't know if the person can be trusted, and you don't want to let down your guard and be vulnerable.

I've seen firsthand the devastation that alcohol and drugs contribute to health and relationships. It's horrible watching someone you love go through such pain and hit such lows.

If you're in a relationship and you know drinking or drugs is an issue, act on this red flag *immediately.*

Red Flag #3: Constant Criticism (Verbal Abuse)

If you're in a relationship with a guy who always criticizes you or talks down to you, not only does this make you feel bad, it can affect your self-esteem and self-worth. Words can be hurtful, and if someone continually throws ugly words of criticism at you, after a while you start to believe it.

You're not born with low self-esteem; it develops over time if you're subjected to put-downs and criticisms on a regular basis. Unfortunately, if you grew up in this kind of negative atmosphere, you're more likely to continue to accept or even attract the same behavior. Don't let this happen! It doesn't have to be that way!

I suggest if you're in a relationship and criticism is an issue, start with having an honest conversation with your partner about how the criticism makes you feel. Let the person know you're hurt by the criticism and it's not okay or acceptable. Set that boundary at the first sign of critical behavior.

Give examples of what the person said and how it made you feel. Be honest and communicate your feelings (which is part of a healthy relationship). If the person refuses to discuss issues or take responsibility, or if the verbal abuse continues, it's a *red flag* that's not going to magically go away. You need to move on from this relationship—unless you're okay with being beaten down with criticism and walking on eggshells the rest of your life. If that's the case, you need to go back and reread Chapter 1: Loving and Respecting Yourself!

Relationship alert:

♥ A healthy relationship does not include ongoing criticism and disrespect.

♥ The longer you stay in a verbally abusive relationship, the more difficult it will be to get out of it and restore your self-esteem.

Red Flag #4: Infidelity

You've probably heard the saying *Once a cheater always a cheater.* That isn't always the case, but it's a tough mental and emotional battle to forgive and trust someone once they've cheated on you.

Cheating happens for different reasons, and some relationships end up being repaired after infidelity. Everyone heals differently.

If you feel you just *can't* forgive his infidelity and it keeps haunting you, this will keep your relationship from moving forward and being healthy.

If you forgive him and he cheats again . . . *run, girl!*

Red Flag #5: Trust Issues/Lying

Great relationships are built on a foundation of trust. Without trust, any kind of relationship will crumble.

Some women think big biceps are sexy, but I think trust is sexy! Trust is a quality I must have in all of my close relationships. If trust isn't there, it's like walking on thin ice all the time and the relationship can't be a deep one, if it's possible at all.

Trust is something that's earned through actions. It's the sense of security that allows both parties to expose themselves fully without any judgments or fears.

You could have personal trust issues because of something that happened in your life that haunts you and you haven't been able to move beyond it or heal from it. What I'm talking about here is geared toward trust issues in a relationship that arise because of your partner's behavior that seems a little shady or inexplicable. For example:

♥ If your date takes you to places that aren't within the local area where you live (yes, I had that happen to me), he might be trying to hide you. This is a *red flag!*

An exception to this might be if you live in a tiny rural town that doesn't have restaurants, movie theaters, etc., and you have to drive a distance for entertainment.

♥ If you're never invited to your guy's house and he's always hanging out at your place, he might be hiding something. This is a *red flag!* Why doesn't he invite you to his house? Does someone else live there? Does he live with his parents? Is it too big of a commitment? Is his place a total mess? Bottomline: You need to find out why he is not inviting you.

♥ If you're dating a guy who doesn't allow photos of the two of you to be posted on social media or doesn't introduce you to family and friends, he may be hiding something. Now if you like to post on Instagram several times a day and video every moment, I understand why a guy wouldn't want to take part, and it could be annoying. I'm talking about an occasional photo of the two of you, showing your relationship to the world! Not allowing any photos to be posted and not introducing you to family and friends is a *red flag.*

Tod and I have a mutual trust, and I attribute our deep level of trust to communicating openly with each other. We talk about everything, and we don't keep secrets from each other. We don't keep passwords secret, we can check each other's emails, and we can both access our financial accounts and social media sites.

If my husband kept passwords a secret, I would wonder why and get suspicious. I would probably go into investigator mode. I think that's human nature. You have to be open and honest to establish trust in a relationship. Once trust is broken, it's hard to earn back.

Real-life example: When Tod and I were dating, we had a conversation about finances. He was honest with me that his credit was not as good as he wanted it to be, which affected his credit score. Being an entrepreneur, he took a few risks, as entrepreneurs often do.

I've always been highly conscious of my credit and proud that I've continuously had a great credit score. I've worked hard on that, and it's important to me. I believe my parents contributed to my frugal behavior with finances. They paid cash for almost everything. If they didn't have the cash for something, they didn't buy it. I believe my dad got his first credit card when he *had* to get one to rent a car.

When I found out that Tod's credit wasn't in great shape, it was kind of a red flag. But instead of immediately judging him and having it be an instant deal breaker, we had an honest conversation about it. I knew this was something he wasn't proud of and was working to correct.

Today, Tod's credit score is higher than mine! It's phenomenal!

Don't be afraid to question your guy on red flags. Have a discussion in person in a nonjudgmental way. Always talk about any important issues in person and not through email or text or over the phone. You want to see his facial expressions and body language because they can tell you a lot (good or bad), even if his words don't. Ask questions in a non-confrontational way. No angry, defensive tone. Then watch the guy's body language. Does the tone of his voice change? Observe and listen carefully. If he acts guilty or defensive, more than likely he's guilty. If he has nothing to hide, he'll be more willing to talk and not resist or get defensive. *Your intuition is usually on target.*

Red Flag #6: Married, Separated, or Noncommittal

When you meet someone who's noncommittal, married, separated, or "in the process" of a divorce, do yourself a favor. Tell him you're interested in pursuing a relationship (if you are), but you won't until he's no longer in a relationship with someone else.

I've witnessed the scenario in which a woman likes a guy and starts dating him while waiting for his divorce to be finalized. Some ladies invest years into the relationship and no divorce. They fall in love—and still no divorce.

Time is our most precious asset. Even one or two years is a lot of time to invest in a relationship that doesn't—and may never—go to the next level. I have a girlfriend who is in a relationship with a noncommittal guy, and this relationship has been going on for a couple of years. My girlfriend keeps saying she wants to move on because the relationship is not going to the next level and she's frustrated, but she won't let go. I always advise her that she deserves much more and encourage her to move on. But I know that she ultimately has to be the one to make that decision.

Why would you want to be a side dish or a dessert? You deserve to be the main course, the full meal. If a guy sincerely cares about you and is serious about pursuing a relationship with you, he'll understand any healthy boundary you set. He should respect your decision not to date him while he's in another relationship or if he's noncommittal. If he doesn't, that will tell you a lot about his character and true intentions.

Setting boundaries just might help speed up the divorce process or noncommittal stage *if* he is indeed serious about continuing a relationship with you.

I don't like this saying, but there's some truth to it: *Why buy the cow when you can get the milk for free?* I know, cheesy. But if a guy is getting exactly what he wants in a relationship and it's easy, chances are he'll continue to get the milk for free as long as he can.

When I met Tod, he was newly divorced. My girlfriend Tricia suggested I ask him to show me his divorce papers. I wouldn't have done that or even thought about it, but after Tricia brought it up, I figured it was probably a good idea. He said he was recently divorced, and he lived in a different state. (We gotta love girlfriends who keep us in check!)

I mustered up the courage and asked to see proof of his divorce—and Tod gladly showed me his divorce decree.

If you have a feeling the person you're dating isn't being honest, don't be afraid to ask questions. Do some digging around if you have to. You have a right to know the truth.

Red Flag #7: Unequal Giving

All relationships take continuous effort. This includes dating as well as relationships with friends, family, and co-workers. All healthy relationships are two-way. They're co-created. It's a balance of give and take. You can't have one person in the relationship putting in 75 percent of the effort and the other person putting in only 25 percent. It might work for awhile, but at some point, the person putting in most of the effort and not seeing much in return will resent the inequity or just get tired of it. *Both parties need a full cup.*

I have seen this kind of trend with one of my friends. When she starts a new relationship, she immediately goes overboard giving, giving, giving. Unfortunately, most of the time, not much is given in return. She gets frustrated, and the relationship doesn't end up working out. She cooks for the man in her life, buys him gifts, makes herself available, and gives 110 percent to the relationship. I think it's her way of wanting to immediately win him over—*and* she's just a giving person by nature. She might temporarily win him over, but what she's doing is setting a precedent right at the beginning of the relationship. She's indicating she's willing to put more into the relationship than what she's receiving. Many men will like that and not bother to reciprocate; but that gets old if you're the giver.

There's nothing wrong with being a giver. I'm a giver and I love giving, but I do expect and need mutual effort.

This is why it's important at the *beginning* of a relationship to set healthy boundaries—expectations of what you're willing to accept and not accept in the relationship. Boundaries are about protecting yourself. I'm not saying to put up walls. If you put up walls, you'll keep everyone out. When expressing boundaries, be clear on what you expect and what you are willing to give in a relationship. Be clear on what you want. Don't be vague with boundaries. Be honest and don't hold back. Lack of boundaries invites lack of respect.

Personal Example of Multiple Red Flags

On one of my first-date experiences, I witnessed multiple red flags. Thank goodness it was just a lunch date because I couldn't leave the restaurant fast enough when we were finished with our meal.

Red flag #1. Right out of the gate, my date was totally rude and talked down to the waiter. Not only was his behavior rude, but it was very embarrassing for me. I felt like crawling under the table and hiding. The waiter didn't deserve to be treated with such disrespect. It wasn't just one disrespectful comment either; it happened throughout our lunch. You can tell a lot about someone's character by how they treat and talk to others, and I didn't like his!

Red flag #2. During our conversation, he told me he didn't like my name. Who tells someone that—on a first date, yet! I thought it was super mean and rude. I was speechless. What do you say when you meet a guy for a first date and he tells you he doesn't like your name?

Red flag #3. Conversation was all about him. This was fine because I didn't want to waste my breath telling him about my life. But it's not a good sign when someone just talks about himself and doesn't bother or care to learn about you.

Needless to say, I didn't waste my time on a second date just to witness more red flags. No thank you!

Discovering Red Flags Through Tough Conversations

Sometimes red flags aren't obvious. A great way to discover them is through having tough conversations early in a relationship.

Tough conversations are those that require you to put on your big girl pants and talk about topics people typically avoid because they're uncomfortable and could trigger conflict. However, these conversations can deepen relationships and reveal potential life partners.

For example, if you think a relationship seems promising, before you make any commitments, you might want to discuss the following issues:

- ♥ Do you both want children? If so, how many children? How soon?

- ♥ Should your children be vaccinated? (This is a hot topic these days and opinions are strong and often unyielding.)

- ♥ Do you want your children to be raised in a religion? If so, which one? What religious holidays will you observe?

- ♥ Do you both want pets? Dog, cat, ferret, bird, or _____? How many?

- ♥ What are your respective five-, ten-, and twenty-year personal and professional goals?

- ♥ Do either of you have a desire to move to a different state or out of the country?

- ♥ Would you want a joint bank account, separate bank accounts, or both?

- ♥ What are your respective political views? (I know if Tod and I weren't on the same page with politics, we'd probably experience tension in our home.) I didn't experience political conflict when I was dating, as political parties seemed to get along much better than they do today. Now, politics could be a hot button.

- ♥ What are your thoughts about roles around the house? Who is going to cook, do laundry, pay the bills?

Don't avoid or change the subject when faced with difficult topics and hope they'll simply disappear because they *will* eventually come up. It's best to not waste time with someone if you uncover a deal breaker. If you do, have the strength and courage to walk away.

Healthy, secure individuals won't be afraid to speak their mind, hang on to what is important to them, and stick to their morals and goals. The idea is to build a solid, honest foundation as a couple so you and your partner can tackle issues and nip them in the bud as they arise.

Green Flags

As much as resolving red flags is critical, spotting and appreciating *green flags* is also important because green flags are signs that you may have found a keeper.

Here are a few of my favorite green flags:

- ♥ He is a good communicator and welcomes open and honest communication.

- ♥ He doesn't play games. He's consistent and doesn't leave you hanging for a few days or go MIA.

- ♥ He's excited and proud to introduce you to his friends and, when appropriate, to his family. He wants to be seen with you.

- ♥ He respects you—your opinions and your morals.

- ♥ You can be yourself with him, without fear of judgment and criticism.

- ♥ His words and actions align.

Take the time and make the effort to inventory the red and green flags as you evaluate a relationship for further investment. Green flags are great, but they can be offset by any one of a number of red flags, not to mention several. The key is to become aware of the red flags and know they're part of that person's character. Then ask yourself if you want to spend more time with him. Typically, people are on their best behavior the first few months of dating, so it may take a while for the person's true colors to appear. Six months of a relationship is normally sufficient to witness a person's real character and behaviors.

Traveling together is the ultimate test. A lot about a person is exposed when traveling, especially if you're not used to spending 24/7 in such close proximity. Sometimes a couple's first trip together will break up a relationship. But think of it this way: You found out that person isn't right for you, and you won't waste any more of your precious time on him.

In the next chapter, I tell the story of my own painful revelation about a man I thought was "the one." In my case, a whole year went by before all his green flags were suddenly canceled by a giant red flag that finally brought the truth to light.

Chapter 4

FROM FAIRY TALE ROMANCE TO SHOCKING REVELATION

You can't go back and change the beginning,
But you can start where you are
and change the ending.
~ C. S. Lewis

Following is one of my most memorable dating stories, but unfortunately I don't mean memorable in a good way!

Mark (I changed his name to protect the guilty) lived in Moraga, California. We were separated by 550 miles—nine hours by car and one and a half hours by plane.

How did this relationship start? Well, I was in charge of planning a large corporate event for the company I worked for in Las Vegas. We were looking for a hotel in Southern California where we could hold the event. I hit it off with the meeting planner at one of the hotels I checked out, and when she discovered I was single, she offered to introduce me to her friend Mark.

The meeting planner gushed about him. She said he was *fun,* he loved to travel, had a great job, and on and on. Wow! It sounded like I needed to meet this Mark guy. So she introduced us via email because he lived in Northern California. We immediately started having phone conversations. (This was before Facetime, Zoom, and all the great technology we have now.) A few weeks went by, and it just so happened Mark was going to be in Las Vegas for a business meeting. Yay! I would get to meet him in person. We were connecting so well during our phone and email conversations that I was excited and looking forward to it.

When I met Mark in the Bellagio Hotel lobby in Las Vegas, I was impressed. He was handsome, well dressed, and had a big smile on his face. We enjoyed a wonderful dinner at Prime Steakhouse in the hotel, dining on the patio with a gorgeous view of the fountains. Our conversation flowed effortlessly. He was easygoing and funny, and I was pleasantly surprised at how well the evening went. Chalk that first date up to a success!

Mark lived in the San Francisco Bay area, which as I mentioned, was 550 miles away. When would we see each other again? I had never had a long-distance relationship, but we connected so well I was willing to give it a try.

We continued our conversations over the phone and via email and text messages. I eagerly looked forward to talking with him and getting to know him better.

During one of our conversations, Mark invited me to a party on a yacht in the San Francisco Bay. That sounded like fun! I had never been on a yacht before. I was in! His personal assistant immediately contacted me to get my information for an airline ticket, and within a few hours, she emailed my flight itinerary. Then *every week* like clockwork after that, I got an email confirmation from Mark's assistant with my booked flight for the weekend.

Yes, I flew from Las Vegas to San Francisco every weekend for one year. My boss at the time kindly let me leave the office a little early on Friday afternoons. The airport was just five minutes from where I worked, and I always boarded the same flight. I'd spend Friday night, Saturday, and most of Sunday at Mark's, then I'd catch the last flight on Sunday evening at 8:50 p.m. and head back home to Las Vegas. For someone who doesn't enjoy flying, I'm amazed I did this for a year!

Friday evening, Mark would be waiting for me outside the airport in his Ferrari, and we'd drive to downtown San Francisco and have dinner at a fabulous restaurant. On Saturday mornings, we typically ate breakfast at a cozy restaurant near his house that served comfort food and great coffee.

Weekends with Mark in the Bay Area were packed with fun and excitement. They usually consisted of bike riding across the Golden Gate Bridge, strolling the streets of Sausalito, shopping in Walnut Creek, eating delicious food, going to Broadway shows, and getting dressed up and going to fundraisers. I enjoyed spending time with him. I was happy and in a great season of life.

We spent Thanksgiving that year in New York City, where he grew up. On Thanksgiving Day, we watched the Macy's Day Parade. We attended *Phantom of the Opera* and the Radio City Rockettes' Christmas Spectacular. I met his brother and mother, and overall, it was a magical holiday.

Mark also had a house in Lake Tahoe, so we went there a few times during the winter months.

As a past president of the Chamber of Commerce and the Rotary Club, Mark was well known and respected in Moraga. He seemed like the whole package, and I thought Mark was *The One* . . . until the dream all came crashing down.

After a year of bliss and fun, the dreaded red flags started showing up. My weekly flights became sporadic and went from every weekend to once or twice a month—and not because *I* wanted them to. Was he seeing someone else so he didn't want me there every weekend? Was he having second thoughts about our relationship? I had no clue.

The weekly routine I'd become accustomed to and looked forward to suddenly changed—but *why?* I wasn't getting any answer from Mark that I believed. When I questioned him and asked why we weren't seeing each other every weekend, he replied that he was busy with a work project . . . that he had to focus and work on the weekends . . . that it would just be temporary. He skillfully and smoothly put me *somewhat* at ease.

Something was off and *I knew it.* I sensed the red flags. They were smothering me, but part of me didn't want to believe it. Everything had been going so well. *What happened?*

I started to not trust him, which caused a lot of uneasiness, especially with our long-distance relationship. On the weekends we didn't spend together, I was constantly wondering what he was doing 550 miles away. I was confused by what was going on, wondering why I wasn't with him. I missed him! Weekends away from Mark were depressing.

Did I do something wrong? Everything seemed so right. This was so sudden, and I didn't see it coming.

Eventually, our disintegrating relationship started seriously getting me down. I wasn't sleeping well, I was sad, I had no appetite and was losing weight, and I started smoking cigarettes. Yes, smoking nasty cigarettes. For some reason, when I felt stressed, cigarettes seemed to calm me down. I don't know if the nicotine actually did that, but it felt like it did at the time.

After I smoked, I'd feel gross because I knew smoking was bad for my skin, teeth, and lungs. Some nights I would sit outside on my patio in Las Vegas at 2 a.m. smoking cigarettes because I couldn't sleep.

Was it something I said? Something I did? Was I not good enough? Not pretty enough? Every insecure thing I could think of tortured my mind.

One weekend I flew to see him. I shouldn't have, but I didn't refuse his offer because if our relationship was going to end, I felt I needed closure. I probably also had the stupid idea that maybe magically things would go back to how they'd been.

We were at his house, and when it began to get dark outside, he scurried around closing all the blinds. He'd never done that before, so it struck me as odd. I also noticed he turned the ringer off on the phone, which also seemed strange. (This was when we still had home phones.)

I noticed more and more red flags, so of course I was feeling paranoid and analyzing his every move that weekend. With this strange behavior, I thought he must be seeing some-one else. I was convinced he was closing the blinds and turning the phone ringer off because this "someone else" might call or see lights on and stop by his house. What else could it be???

I questioned Mark a lot that weekend, and he denied anything out of the ordinary was going on. Maybe I was just a crazy paranoid woman. . . .

Sunday morning, when Mark was in the garage getting the bikes ready for a ride across the Golden Gate Bridge, I heard another male voice. Mark was talking to someone in the garage, so I opened the door from the kitchen to the garage. He quickly asked me to please close the door, saying he was having a private conversation. I went inside and immediately put my ear up against the door, trying to hear. Although I couldn't hear exactly what they were saying, I could tell the conversation got a little heated. When the mysterious guy left, Mark didn't want to talk about the conversation when I asked him about it. He said it was work related, that he was talking to a client, and it was no big deal.

We started to not spend much time at his house on the weekends. A lot of our activities were elsewhere, and one weekend, we even stayed at a hotel in the city. Mark also visited me a few times in Las Vegas, which wasn't the norm. I had always flown to San Francisco on the weekends.

Now let's go back in time to a mysterious question Mark had asked me before things started falling apart—back when our relationship felt solid, *before* all of the red flags started popping up.

One evening, Mark and I were talking in the hot tub and he asked me a question that seemed a little strange at the time. I didn't think much about it, but in retrospect, I can see how it related to the red flags.

That evening in the hot tub, Mark asked me, "If you were in love with someone and they asked you to leave the country with them and not have contact ever again with your family or anyone you knew, would you do it?"

It didn't take me long to answer: "Oh hell no!" My response basically squashed that question, and we just moved on with our conversation.

Now back to real time in our relationship:

On a Sunday evening, I boarded my flight home from San Francisco to Las Vegas, the way I'd done many times over the past year. I didn't know it at the time, but that would be the last flight I would take home from Mark's—and the last time I would see him . . . ever again.

Several weeks went by. We talked on the phone, but I was getting fed up with his new secret life. I immersed myself in work and other activities to keep busy so I could move on from this relationship that was clearly on the verge of ending. I still had no solid clue why. I was experiencing a roller coaster of emotions.

Then, one day Mark made Bay Area newspaper headlines, and I got the news from a friend of a friend who lived there.

Mark's house had been raided by the FBI. They confiscated his computers and files, and he was under investigation for running a Ponzi scheme. Instead of investing his clients' funds as promised, he had been depositing their money in his personal bank account and spending it on homes, cars, and lavish trips.

Everything suddenly made sense. Mark had been living the high life built on dishonest gains, and apparently it had come crashing down on him during the past few months.

I'd convinced myself he was cheating on me, but I had no clue he'd been cheating many people out of their life savings and retirement funds! Our relationship ending had nothing to do with me personally. It had to do with him being a thief!

Mark made bail and a trial date was set.

He called me several times and I didn't answer my phone. He left messages telling me he was innocent and it was all a misunderstanding.

But … I. WAS. DONE. I was devastated and knew it was time to close the door on the relationship—and *nail the door shut.*

The next few months were super painful for me. I felt as if I'd just spent a whole year of my life with a person I didn't really know.

I made it through work weeks and basically hibernated on the weekends. My girlfriends would drop by and try to snatch me up to go out for dinner or drinks, but I wanted time to be alone. I needed time to be sad, time to be mad, time to realize I deserve more than this guy who was clearly *not* "The One." This was a dark season for me. I couldn't see even a tiny speck of light at the end of the tunnel.

Then I found out through the same friend of a friend that Mark had fled before his court date. Now he was a fugitive.

Circle back with me to that late night conversation in the hot tub when Mark asked me if I would *leave the country for someone I loved and not have contact with anyone I knew again.* Was he planning his escape back then because he knew he was on the brink of being caught? Was he curious if I would be in for the ride? Was he questioning the depth of my love for him? I don't know, of course, but that conversation haunted me for some time. I'm extremely grateful I wasn't vulnerable to playing along with him.

Looking back on this relationship, not only was it heart breaking, but it could have been extremely dangerous for me. Apparently, a few of his clients caught on that he wasn't investing their money as he said he was. I'm fairly sure that's what the conversation in the garage was all about that he didn't

want me to hear. A lot of people became angry with him—
and justifiably! Most of them had invested their life savings
with him, and their money was gone! I could have easily been
caught in the middle of revenge against him. I wish I would
have acted more wisely and quickly on the red flags because of
what *could have* happened.

To top it off, I felt guilty! The lavish dinners, gifts, events,
shopping, and luxuries I had enjoyed with Mark were basically
from money stolen from innocent people. Most of them were
older folks who thought they were investing their life savings
for retirement. This made me feel horrible, but I knew I couldn't
carry that guilt with me because I wasn't aware of what he was
doing. I believed he had a successful business.

This, my friends, was a tough season for me—but I made
it through with the help of God, friends, family, co-workers,
and a positive mindset. I knew I deserved better. I learned
valuable lessons and came out of this relationship a stronger
woman than before. Plus, I racked up a lot of frequent
flier miles!

What happened to Mark? He was arrested two years after
being on the run and sentenced to seven years in prison.

Chapter 5

HEALTHY LIFESTYLE = HEALTHY RELATIONSHIPS

*Healthy habits are learned in the same way
as unhealthy ones – through practice.*
~ Wayne Dyer

Let's take a break from red flags and consider *healthy* relationships—including the one you have with *yourself.* It's a privilege to be alive and healthy, so why wouldn't you want to do everything possible to maintain a healthy lifestyle, body, and mind? What a great gift to give yourself and a partner—*a healthy you!* Consider that lack of health can, and usually does, have detrimental effects on your personal happiness as well as the quality of your relationships.

In the previous chapter, I admitted that cigarettes were a solace for me when I was stressed out—but in retrospect, that was *not* a good choice. Smoking was never a daily habit for me, but it somehow provided a distraction during stressful times. Thank goodness I didn't have tons of stress in my life.

Taming Stress

Over the years, I've learned to take control of my mind and actions during stressful situations. Now I have healthy strategies to support me. Instead of grabbing a cigarette or a drink, or letting stress take over and blurting out ugly words, I can overcome stress. I take a deep breath without immediately reacting. I pray, exercise, or talk about whatever is on my mind to my husband, friends, or family. I honor my health and body and will never let myself go back down the road of letting stress take over or get out of control. Instead of unhealthy reactions that will only make the situation worse, I think about how I am going to react. Knowing that stress is related to a lot of illnesses and disease is reason enough to nip it in the bud and figure out healthy ways to let it go.

   Single KNOW More

When you're stressed, I highly recommend you not rely on cigarettes, alcohol, drugs, and toxic relationships to ease the pain. You have only one body, so best to take great care of it. You can't go and buy another one.

Developing Healthy Lifestyle Habits

Your health depends not only on releasing stress in good ways, but on what you eat, watch, listen to, and read, and the people you choose to have in your life.

Many people are unhealthy due to harmful lifestyle habits. Don't wait until you start having symptoms of ill health to make good choices. Never take your health for granted.

Unfortunately, sometimes it takes a setback for us to fully appreciate our health. I know when I'm not feeling well—if I have a cold or I'm just not feeling 100 percent—I want to feel better, have energy, and get back to my normal self and routine as soon as I can. In those moments I look at health differently and appreciate it much more.

Living a healthy lifestyle has many benefits. For example, you will:

- age well, which generally means you look and feel younger and can do more activities without pain, weakness, or tiredness;

- have a stronger immune system;

- feel more confident;

- be happier;

♥ attract people who also hold healthy lifestyle values.

Worth it—right? But what does a healthy lifestyle include? Basically, it means:

♥ eating healthy,

♥ exercising,

♥ balancing work with the rest of your life,

♥ managing your stress,

♥ having a positive mindset,

♥ doing things that make you feel good, and

♥ getting adequate sleep.

A healthy lifestyle is not just another diet or working out seven days a week. It's a combination of healthy habits and actions that you do on a consistent basis so it becomes routine. When you eat healthy food consistently or work out consistently, your body starts to crave it. A lot of times people will be consistent for one or two weeks or maybe a month and then give up and go back to old habits. It takes focus, grit, and determination to stay on track, but it gets easier and more automatic as time goes on.

Each day when you wake up, you have a "blank slate." You control what is "written" on that slate through your choices. For instance, did you know that your day is influenced by how you spend the first hour? How are you waking up? Are you filling your mind immediately with negative news or social media? Or are you reading positive, uplifting books, praying, or just sitting quietly having a cup of coffee or tea? The first approach will give the day an underlying angst and things may not go well. The second will supply underlying peace and harmony, which generally will give your day the same enjoyable vibe.

Not every day is going to be perfect, of course. If you fall off the wagon (which we all do!), you have the opportunity to make better choices when you get out of bed the next day. If you eat that quart of mint chip ice cream or bag of potato chips, don't beat yourself up for days; just choose not to do it again. Or, you could choose to moderate your snacks by eating less and perhaps spreading them out over the week.

Many people want the end result of being healthy or at their ideal weight, but they aren't willing or don't have the discipline to do the consistent work it takes to get there. Develop a plan and stick to it until you see enough results to further motivate you.

What You Put IN Your Body

Over the past ten years, I have become more health conscious than ever before. Tod and I don't even keep Advil or aspirin in our *wellness* cabinet. We are consistent about exercising and taking our vitamins daily. We eat organic as much as possible and very little processed food. These are just a few life choices Tod and I make to help keep our bodies and minds healthy and operating at their best for as long as we possibly can.

My own weakness is carbs—bread, crackers, pasta, potato chips.... But I know that feeding my body whatever tastes good, such as yummy sugar and carbs, won't help me accomplish my goals.

I think once you start being mindful of what you eat—the ingredients in food and their effects on your body—you'll become more conscious about what you eat and look at the ingredients list on products before purchasing them. I do.

I love to eat at restaurants (and get served!). I could literally eat Mexican food several times a week. I love nachos, guacamole, salsa, tacos, enchiladas, beans and rice. . . . *Yum!* I love it all!

That said, Tod and I cook most of our meals at home. This, of course, requires time and energy, but we eat healthier meals, and we know exactly how they're prepared. For us, the extra effort of cooking at home is worth the health benefits.

What You Put ON Your Body

Not only do you need to be conscious about what you put in your mouth but also about the products you put *on your* body. Many products contain harmful ingredients. Once you start doing a little research about the ingredients in makeup, perfume, body wash, toothpaste, deodorant, and even nail polish, you'll be shocked that you've been applying these chemicals directly on your body.

I would like to share some of my healthy lifestyle tips, in no particular order. They may help you become more aware of what you could change to support your own health and happiness.

Healthy Tip #1: Use Sunscreen and Hydrate Your Skin.

Most of the visible skin changes associated with premature aging are avoidable, because most of the damage has one cause—the sun's ultraviolet (UV) rays. Exposure to the sun can cause wrinkles, pigmentation, sunspots, reduced skin elasticity, and skin cancer.[4]

I've always been quite careful about taking care of my skin from head to toe. In my twenties, I lived in Las Vegas, so I had to get in the habit of applying sunscreen and moisturizing my body daily, because the climate is excessively sunny and dry. Living where it's abundantly sunny makes it impossible to avoid the sun. Besides, I enjoy the sun and I'm thankful I live in a great climate—so I'm not a total sun party pooper. I just make sure to protect my skin as much as I can. This includes always wearing a cap when exercising outside and wearing my larger cute hats with big brims when out in the sun for an extended time. At the beach or poolside, I stay underneath an umbrella as much as possible. I apply at least an SPF 30 sunscreen on my face and all other body parts exposed to the sun.

Remember to apply sunscreen to your hands, neck, and chest as well. These areas are the first to show signs of aging, so protect them! It's much easier to *prevent* sun damage than repair it.

As part of my daily routine, I apply sunscreen to my face after applying moisturizer and before makeup. I recommend using a sunscreen that's formulated specifically for the face because it's noncomedogenic, which means it doesn't clog your pores and cause breakouts. Facial sunscreen costs more, but if you're just applying it to your face and neck, it will last longer than if you're using it on other parts of your body as well. Plus, it takes only a small amount of product.

Be aware that while driving, sun coming through the car's windshield and windows can contribute to sun damage on your face, hands, neck, chest, arms, or any uncovered area of your skin. People who drive a lot will see more sun damage on the left side of their face because it's exposed to the sun coming through the driver's side window.

Okay, I agree it's more fun to live in the moment and soak up the sun. However, I urge you to think about the skin damage you'll see five to ten years down the road—not to mention the increased risk of skin cancer. Moderate sun and the vitamin D benefits are healthy, but don't overdo a good thing. Today, natural-looking spray tans or tanning lotions are available for special occasions or whenever you want a bronze boost.

I've seen women not think twice about lounging in the sun every chance they get. They just love the look of a deep dark tan and seem more than willing to damage their skin to achieve it. A glowing tan looks great, but it's just not worth all of the sun damage that comes with it. Personally, I've invested too much into skin care treatments and skin care products to have sun damage take over—and it can take over quickly!! SPF is my BFF.

In my early thirties, I had my first eye-opening experience with aging skin. I was on a flight from Las Vegas (where I lived at the time) to Iowa (where I grew up), traveling to visit my parents. As the airplane was preparing to land, I pulled out a little mirror from my purse to check my makeup. When I looked in the mirror, I was horrified at how my neck looked! Whose neck was that?! I noticed wrinkles I'd never noticed

                    Single KNOW More

before. I immediately applied some moisturizer I had in my purse and tried to plump up my skin.

The air in airplanes is super dry and can suck the life out of skin—as it did to my neck. Therefore, it doesn't surprise me that I experienced my first frightening sign of aging on an airplane.

Now before traveling, I hydrate well inside and out. Because I dislike using the restroom on a plane, I drink lots of water two hours before flying. That way, I make most of my trips to the restroom before I board the flight. Then, on the flight, I just sip water. I also generously apply moisturizer from head to toe.

One of my favorite traveling tips is facial mist. I carry a small bottle in my purse to meet airline requirements. Several times during a flight I spritz my face, hands, and neck to help keep my skin hydrated.

On long flights at nighttime, hydrating eye patches are a good option.

Happy traveling!

Healthy Tip #2: Be Organized.

When my office desk is organized, it feels good. When my house is clean and organized, I feel more at ease. When things are tidy and clean, I can find what I need and it's good for my mood.

So yes, keeping your surroundings (home/workspace) clean and organized is part of living a healthy lifestyle. You will feel more productive, and your day will flow more easily.

Here are a few things you can do to make that happen:

♥ Make your bed first thing in the morning. This takes only a few minutes.

♥ Don't wake up to a sink full of dirty dishes (not a motivating sight in the morning!). Make sure your kitchen is clean and organized before going to bed.

♥ Don't let laundry overflow until you don't have any clean undies and you have mounds of laundry to do all at once. Do a few loads in pockets of free time or multitasking. Or, choose a day of the week— maybe Saturday or Sunday—to get caught up on laundry for the week.

♥ Stay on track with a to-do list. Like me, I'm sure you have a lot going on, and it's difficult to impossible to remember everything! The best way to stay on track is to immediately add whatever task pops into your mind to your to-do list. Keep all your notes in one place, because otherwise (if you're like I was), you'll have various notepads and sticky notes with reminders everywhere! You might want to keep your list on your phone, for example.

♥ Brighten up a room and your mood with fresh flowers. Studies have shown that flowers can contribute to creative energy and positive vibes, making us feel better. Another benefit of flowers is that they reduce stress.[5] Who knew flowers were so beneficial to our health?! Flowers don't have to be expensive. I typically buy flowers at Trader Joe's.

   Single KNOW More

You can buy a dozen roses or other colorful bouquets
for under $15. A couple of my favorites are hydran-
geas and peonies. I love buying them when they're
in season, and when my favorites aren't in season,
my typical go-to is white roses or red for a pop of
color. I add bouquets of fresh flowers to both our
home and office.

♥ Have a bowl of fresh lemons on hand as well,
because citrus juice can also be uplifting and boost
energy. Most mornings Tod and I drink a glass
of warm lemon water before coffee.

Healthy Tip #3: Get Your Beauty Sleep.

A healthy lifestyle includes getting a good night's sleep,
which plays an important role in your physical health. Sleep
is involved in the healing and repair of your heart and blood
vessels. When you're sleeping, your immune system is stron-
gest. Ongoing sleep deficiency is linked to an increased risk
of heart disease, kidney disease, high blood pressure, diabetes,
and stroke.[6]

All that should be reason enough to get adequate sleep!

Sleep requirements vary slightly from person to person,
but most healthy adults need between seven and nine hours
of sleep a night to function at their best. (I personally like
seven to eight hours of sleep.) Good sleep is important at
any age.

I've never been a night owl. I'm more energetic and
productive in the morning. I usually find myself hitting a

wall late in the afternoon, and my productive, creative juices seem to fade. I take advantage of my morning energy to complete tasks. Then if I do hit a wall in the afternoon, I feel good about having gotten a lot accomplished the first half of the day.

When are you most energetic? Are you making the most of your time to be productive when you have the most energy?

I've always made it a priority to get adequate sleep, even when I was single. I rarely stayed out late. I usually lived by the general rule that "nothing good ever happens after midnight." Of course occasionally I ignored the midnight rule, but it didn't happen very often.

To help relax your mind and get ready for restful sleep, it's best not to talk about negative things or watch negative or violent TV shows before going to sleep at night. Before Tod and I go to bed, I will sometimes have to catch myself before I bring up something negative that I read on social media or saw on the news earlier in the day. I'm good now about keeping those thoughts and conversations for another time.

If I'm having a restless night and my mind is darting around thinking of things I need to do, or if I'm just not tired, I use lavender essential oil to relax me. I rub a few drops of the oil behind my ears and on the back of my neck. Then I inhale two to three times where I put the drops of oil on the palm of my hand.

I also keep melatonin on hand, which is produced by your body naturally and helps with sleep. Any supplementation of melatonin is meant for short-term or occasional use. Do your research or ask your doctor to find out if it's a good option for you. I'm not qualified to give medical advice; I'm just suggesting a product you can buy in the supplement section at stores that works for me. Another natural sleep product to research that works for some people is valerian root.

Speaking of beauty sleep, make sure to keep your bedding clean. Daily use causes a buildup of oils, dirt, and sweat on your bedding. This buildup can harbor bacteria, which in turn can make your skin break out. I love getting in bed at night and snuggling into fresh, clean sheets!

Getting a good night's sleep is part of my healthy lifestyle and a factor I attribute to my great health and aging gracefully. I highly recommend it.

Healthy Tip #4: Exercise.

Exercise is critical for a healthy lifestyle. Only about one in five adults and teens get enough exercise to maintain good health.[7] Exercise is defined as any movement that makes your muscles work and requires your body to burn calories. It provides both physical and mental health benefits. For example, exercise:

- ♥ increases energy;
- ♥ helps fight depression;
- ♥ can help with relaxation and sleep quality; and
- ♥ aids weight loss.

If you don't have an exercise routine, the simplest way to get moving and improve your health is to start walking. It's free, easy, and can be done just about anywhere.

Exercising consistently can be tough. Honestly, I rarely say, "Woohoo, I get to exercise!" Most of the time, I have to push myself, or Tod gives me a little push, or I push him. We work well together, motivating each other. Having an accountability partner certainly helps when exercising.

When I was single, I didn't have a consistent accountability partner, so I enjoyed going to group classes at the gym. This worked out great for me because I'd go to the gym after work and be in a healthy environment with other humans, not in my apartment alone. Now I prefer to work out first thing in the morning, before I start my workday.

The more you sit around and do nothing active (working on the computer, scrolling through social media, or watching TV), the more you resist being active. You get *lazy*. But if you get up and move, then energy begins to flow.

Tod and I always aim to walk after dinner rather than get sucked into sitting on the sofa watching TV. Going for a walk after a meal does a lot for your body. It boosts metabolism, improves digestion, lowers stress levels, and boosts blood flow.[8]

I will continue exercising for as long as I can to help maintain a healthy body and mind! Exercise is a must for a healthy lifestyle. There are so many forms of exercise, I'm sure you can find a few you enjoy, so get moving and reap the benefits!

Healthy Tip #5: Drink Water (Hydrate).

Drinking adequate water is probably the easiest thing to do, but not many people drink the recommended amount. I admit most days I don't drink enough water.

Drinking water each day is crucial for many reasons. Water:

♥ regulates body temperature;

♥ keeps joints lubricated;

♥ prevents infections;

♥ delivers nutrients to cells;

♥ keeps organs functioning properly;

♥ is helpful for weight loss; and

♥ improves sleep quality and mood.[9]

To make water taste better, I simply add fresh fruit juice, such as lemon or lime, to give it a little burst of flavor. Or, I add a sprig of rosemary and lemon slices to a bottle of water and keep it in the fridge for a day or so to enhance the flavors.

I mentioned that Tod and I add fresh squeezed lemon to a glass of warm water and drink it almost every morning. One reason is that drinking warm lemon water on an empty stomach helps flush out toxins. In addition, lemon water gives your immune system a boost, aids digestion, reduces inflammation, and is great for an energy boost![10]

Drinking a cup of water before a meal can help you feel fuller and help prevent overeating. How easy is that! Give it a try and see if it works for you.

Healthy Tip #6: Have an Attitude of Gratitude.

Start each day with a grateful heart. When you wake up in the morning, instead of grabbing your phone and becoming consumed with email, social media, or news, lie in bed for a minute or two. Take time to express gratitude for the opportunity to be alive. When you own your morning, you control your day.

When I wake up, I like to say, "Thank you, God, for another day. Thank you for my health, thank you for my loving husband, thank you for my family, thank you for our thriving business. Please guide me to make wise decisions today and be an example to others." I pray to be an example to others because I believe everyone needs encouragement.

Here's an interesting fact: "When we express and receive gratitude, our brain releases serotonin and dopamine, the two crucial neurotransmitters responsible for our emotions, and they make us feel 'good.' They enhance our mood immediately, making us feel happy from the inside."[11]

The next time you're feeling even a little bit down, count your blessings!

Healthy Tip #7: Do Acts of Kindness.

It's amazing how acts of kindness create wonderful feelings. When I do acts of kindness, it fills me with joy—and sometimes even tears of joy.

Following are a few examples of how Tod and I show kindness and help contribute to our community:

- ♥ During the holiday season, we love to bless others. We give people who didn't have such a great year a little extra cash or gift cards.

- ♥ We purchase $50 Costco gift cards, and when we're shopping in Costco, we randomly give out the gift

 Single KNOW More

cards. (We usually choose families with just essentials in their cart.)

- ♥ When dining at restaurants, we pick a random table and secretly pay their check. It's so fun when the waitress or waiter tells them their meal has been paid for by an anonymous guest. They start looking around trying to figure out who it is. The last time, we did this for two elderly women having lunch.

- ♥ We donate a percentage of our business's income to homeless families.

When I have the chance to show kindness or help someone and I miss the opportunity, it bothers me. One day when Tod and I were checking out at Costco with our usual cartful of goodies, I didn't notice the guy standing behind us. As we were walking out of the store, Tod mentioned we should have let the guy check out before us because he had only one item (a rotisserie chicken). Plus, we should have added the chicken to our order and paid for it. I immediately agreed and felt sad. Thoughts started running through my mind: *Was he buying only a chicken because that was all he could afford? Was he taking it home for dinner to feed his family? Maybe he could have afforded more groceries but just wanted that one chicken at the time.* I'll never know the real story, but I felt terrible and wished I would have been more aware and noticed him in line so I could have given him a blessing—whether he needed it or not.

Small efforts can create big impacts—and blessings go both ways. Express your feelings and let people know when they've made an impact in your life. It makes people feel good knowing they've been helpful and made a difference. They aren't mind readers, so if you don't tell them, they will never know.

Small gestures can make people feel thought of and special. Who doesn't like that? Following are actions you can take to let people know you care about them:

- ♥ When you notice on social media that it's someone's birthday, wish them a happy birthday. (I know it puts a smile on my face.)

- ♥ Hug your loved ones more and tell them you love them. Don't just assume they know. When you say "I love you," you're saying I'm here for you. We're never promised tomorrow. Show your feelings and make your loved ones feel special today.

- ♥ Listen when someone is talking to you. Put down your phone, stop what you're doing, and listen. I catch myself sometimes half listening to my husband, and I can tell it irritates him, just as it irritates me when he is distracted and isn't fully listening to me. When people are talking to us, they deserve our full attention.

- ♥ Prepare a loved one's favorite meal. If you're preparing it for a significant other, every once in a while make it romantic and fun: Add flowers and candles to the table, and put on soothing music.

Eating at home doesn't have to be boring.

Tod and I both love to be massaged, so we often massage each other's shoulders, legs, and arms. He loves to have me run my fingers through his hair and massage his scalp. Such simple, small gestures can make your significant other feel loved and connected.

Think about it, and I'm sure you can come up with many ways to show people you love and care about them. It can cost nothing and take a small amount of effort with significant returns.

Healthy Tip #8: Don't Smoke, and Limit Alcohol Consumption.

I mentioned in an earlier chapter, I used to smoke cigarettes during my single years when I went through stressful times. Most of my stress stemmed from dating or sometimes my job, but thank goodness I didn't experience a lot of it. Smoking for me was a random, off-and-on, stress-related habit.

I kicked the nasty cigarette habit for good when I started dating Tod. I didn't quit because I no longer had stress in my life, but because I learned healthier ways to deal with stress. Now, when stress pops up in my life, I tackle it by looking for solutions. I turn any negative thoughts to positive thoughts and don't dwell on and get stuck in whatever is creating the stress. I turn a lot over to God, because I can control only so much, and God's great wisdom can help resolve stressful situations.

Among youth, vaping is more popular than any tradition-al tobacco product. Vaping may be somewhat less harmful than smoking, but it still presents serious health dangers.[12]

Quitting smoking is one of the best things you can do for your health. Smoking harms nearly every organ in your body, including your heart.

I've also learned over the years it is wise to limit alcohol intake. You will rarely see my social media pages displaying alcohol or me drinking alcohol. I have witnessed how addicting alcohol can be and the long-term effects of alcohol on loved ones.

We are what we repeatedly do. Excellence, then,
is not an act but a habit.
~ Aristotle

I hope this chapter has inspired you to uplevel your health, even if it's by adding one or two of the suggested tips at a time that you don't yet do until they become habits. A healthy body and mind contribute greatly to happiness—and attracting healthy, happy significant others.

Now let's move on and consider why you shouldn't settle for less!

Chapter 6

DON'T SETTLE – YOU DESERVE MORE

Being single doesn't mean you're weak.
It means you're strong enough to wait
for what you deserve.
~ Niall Horan

What exactly does "settling" mean? It means accepting less than you want, because you don't believe you can *get* what you want. I believe settling is a choice made from fear or maybe laziness or not feeling worthy. Underlying that choice is a limiting belief. If you don't believe you can have what you want or don't think you deserve it, you'll settle for less.

Settling doesn't just apply to dating; it applies to all areas of your life. People settle for less than they want in:

- ♥ relationships,
- ♥ jobs,
- ♥ income, and
- ♥ health.

When it comes to dating and marriage, women settle for many reasons. If you settle, you're likely to regret that decision in the long run—or even in the short run.

It's best not to rush or force relationships. After all, you can't force someone to love you or want to marry you. Not only is trying exhausting, but you're setting yourself up for failure.

It's important to invest time and energy in finding the right partner to be with for life. Now I'm not saying there are 100-percent-perfect men out there or that relationships should be 100 percent perfect. That's not realistic. Everyone has flaws, weaknesses, and quirkiness. You shouldn't be seeking perfection, but don't lower your standards or sacrifice what's important to you. Never settle for less than you deserve—and everyone deserves respect and love. Your partner should be an asset in your life, not a liability.

I believe we all have deal breakers when seeking a relationship, and deal breakers are a reason not to settle, which is why they're called deal *breakers*. For example, you may be into health, and a deal breaker would be smoking. You may want to have children, and a deal breaker would be not wanting children. It's wise to know what your deal breakers are so you won't settle for someone who's not going to fulfill what you want. . . . And don't count on someone changing!

So why do some women settle?

♥ *Some settle because they simply get tired of the dating scene.* I experienced this and can relate. Around the age of forty, I started to not enjoy going out to bars or clubs on the weekends. I didn't enjoy dating as much as I did in my twenties and thirties, although I never enjoyed the bar scene. I felt myself hitting a wall. I was starting to see a lot of the same people out every weekend, and the age vibe was kicking in.

   If you start dating when you're sixteen and are still dating when you're thirty-five, you've been dating for more than half your life, and that can feel like a long time. In some cases that's a lot of dates and effort!

   However, reaching a certain age and wanting to get out of the dating scene is not a reason to settle. I realized I needed to find other ways to meet men who were more age appropriate.

♥ *Some settle because they have baby fever.* When women hit a certain age, they realize the window for having a baby is getting smaller. They start feeling an urgency to have a baby if they want one.

When women get to approximately their late thirties, their chance of getting pregnant starts to narrow. However, most *men* are capable of fathering babies into their fifties and sixties! Such a huge age gap between women and men when it comes to fertility is a mystery. Dating and relationships might be easier if we all had the same biological clock. But God had His reasons for this when He created man and woman.

I have no children. I love children and I never imagined I wouldn't be a mother. For some reason, though, having children wasn't part of my life's journey. At this point in my life, I've accepted it and believe not having children happened for a reason. Again, I'm trusting God's plan.

If you are meant to have a baby or babies, it will happen. I urge you not to rush a relationship or marry the wrong person to *make* it happen. Bringing children into a relationship that's not solid will put even more strain on the relationship, and that's not fair to a child who may have to suffer the consequences.

In addition, wanting children to try to make a relationship better or keep a man in your life is unhealthy and never a good idea.

♥ *Some settle because they think they may not find anyone better.* Why would you have the belief that you can't find someone better? With that mindset and belief, you won't. Change your mindset! You deserve a man who fulfills your desires and needs. Stay positive. Your thoughts and beliefs are powerful. You will attract what you focus on and think you deserve. Having a relationship is a lot of work, and when you're not with the right person, it's even harder.

Lessons from Experience

I was the queen of first dates. I wasn't going to settle. If I was on a date and I started thinking about being at home in my comfy pj's cuddled on the sofa with a blanket, I knew it wasn't a good sign. If I was into a guy, he would have my full attention.

Feeling the Chemistry

After a first date, if you don't feel any chemistry or connection and you're not excited to see the person again, you may not want to invest time in a second date. This isn't the case 100 percent of the time, but for me, it was true about 99 percent of the time. I knew almost right away if we had a good connection.

I hope you won't go on a date just because you have nothing better to do or for a free dinner and drinks. That's not only a waste of *your* time, but you're not being fair to the person investing *his* time.

What became monotonous for me when I dated was the typical first-date conversation about my life: where I grew up, how many siblings I have, where I went to school, my career, my hobbies. I got tired of relating my basic life details over and over and over again. It got to the point where it felt robotic or more like a job interview than a date.

My mom always loved hearing about my dates and just wanted her little girl to find a great man. She lived in Iowa and we visited on the phone every weekend to chat and catch up. I was thirty-six when my mom suddenly passed away. I wish she could have met my husband Tod. She'd love him and be so thankful that I'm happy and I've finally found my life partner!

For the Right Reasons

Do you know someone who settled for financial values versus relationship values? There's a nickname for that kind of woman: It's called *gold digger*. That's someone who only likes people because of their net worth, or because of what they own.

Just to be clear, there's nothing wrong with desiring a man who is financially stable. In fact, that was one of my own criteria when I was dating. I had a good job, owned a home, and drove a nice car, and I expected the same from guys I dated. But that wasn't the *only* qualifier.

If financial status/gain is your main goal or value in a relationship, you need to go back and reread Chapter 1, Loving and Respecting Yourself.

Yes, having an abundance of money can be fun and make for more opportunities and maybe a little less stress, but a good, solid relationship isn't based on financial status alone.

In fact, money can cause a lot of destruction in relationships. If you want a relationship for monetary gain only, you'll be cheating yourself out of many other aspects of a healthy, loving relationship. For example, it's ideal to have honest communication and a respectful, supportive connection. You'll want to motivate each other to be better, laugh together, and grow together—to enjoy each other's company so you want to spend time together. You'll want a best friend and a trusted partner.

I recommend *not* marrying a sugar daddy who's twenty-five years older than you and old enough to be your father. The guy you're dating shouldn't be a daddy figure or the daddy you always wanted. Sorry, but that has a red flag waving all over it.

Money buys a lot of things, but it doesn't buy true love or long-term happiness. This is evident from the headlines about famous or highly successful people battling depression, infidelity, low self-esteem, and drug and alcohol abuse, and even committing suicide. Money can in fact *magnify* tough situations, so when talking about money, open and honest communication is a must.

Being in a relationship for the right reasons will give you more inner and outer peace, stability, confidence, and the possibility for a healthy, lasting union.

I know how finances can cause aggravation and emotions in (or outside of) a relationship. For this reason, Tod and I made an agreement when it comes to purchases: Any purchase over a certain dollar amount is a decision we make together; any purchase below that limit we can make wisely on our own. I do have to say Tod has broken this rule when buying me gifts—but I let that slide. LOL

Fear Not and Know Thyself

Some women are in wrong relationship after wrong relationship because they don't like to be alone or they fear they'll end up single all their life. They don't give *themselves* time in between relationships to be alone and get the relationship with themselves healthy and strong, mentally and physically. One week they post a photo of the man of their dreams; then the next week they post a different man of their dreams. This just makes them look desperate.

It's healthy to experience alone time and get to know yourself and what makes you happy. Take time and reflect on the last relationship you had that ended and analyze why it didn't work. Decide what you can do differently in your next relationship. Maybe some alone time will help you learn things about yourself you never knew. It's not fair to the next guy if you jump into the new relationship carrying baggage from your previous relationship. First, you need to *empty your griefcase.* Work on yourself so you can begin a new relationship with a healed, open heart and mind. Take time to experience how independence feels. It doesn't always feel great, and it can get lonely, but it can also feel refreshing and rewarding.

When I was single, I actually enjoyed living by myself and having alone time, even though I also love companionship. After a breakup, I needed breakup detox time to reflect and go through all the different emotions that arise after a break-up. These emotions might be:

- ♥ heartbreak,

- ♥ sadness,

- ♥ loneliness,

- ♥ anger, or

- ♥ not feeling worthy.

Don't avoid feeling your emotions. You need to flush them out and set them free so you can move forward with a clear head and heart. If you don't release breakup emotions, they'll come out on their own at some point. The sooner you feel and free them the better. Detox your mind and refresh your heart.

Change Him? Don't Even Try

Important: Don't settle and think you can eventually *change* someone.

As much as we would all like to believe we can change someone, it's more than likely not going to happen unless you have superpowers. You might be a good persuader and persuade someone to change something, but it will probably be a temporary mask to a current situation or to get what that person wants. You won't be able to change someone who doesn't see an issue with their actions or words. Trying to change a guy could actually push him away, or he might feel resentful. No one changes permanently unless *they* choose to. You can beg them or shame them, but only one thing makes someone change: They realize they need to.

No Commitment?

Another tip: Don't settle if you don't get a commitment within a reasonable time. No point in chasing that dream.

Are you putting all your relationship efforts in one basket for someone who won't commit? Or someone who dates other people as well as you? The saying "Don't put all your eggs in one basket" applies to relationships and a lot of other areas in life. *He* may want many baskets, but if you're looking for a stable committed relationship, don't put all your eggs in *his* basket. Either he's not ready or he's the wrong one.

If you aren't getting the commitment you want after dating for a while, why would you give all your time and effort to the relationship? Don't always be available and on demand. If you're right for each other, that person will want to commit—and want you to commit as well.

My friends, if he says he's too busy to make time to see you, too busy to call you, or too busy to send a text (which takes one minute), or goes MIA, *he's not that into you.*

We all make time for what's important to us. Sometimes it takes losing what we were settling for or thought we wanted to remind us that we deserve better.

I know from experience, when certain types of behavior show up in a relationship, more than likely it won't end up working out. And in those cases, consider yourself lucky!

When red flags start showing up, you'll feel it in your gut. Don't waste your time and settle. Time is our most precious commodity. Focus it on relationships that make you feel good and people who appreciate you.

It's better to be just you than you with Mr. Wrong.

Where and how do you meet Mr. Right? We'll address that in Chapter 7.

Chapter 7

WHERE TO MEET YOUR DREAM GUY – SAFELY

*A boy and a girl started dating after
he backed his car into hers.
They met by accident.
~ Adam Young*

The million-dollar question: *Where are all the good men?* Chances are, the man of your dreams isn't going to come knocking on your door or just fall into your arms. Neither will you find him by sitting home scrolling through social media or watching Netflix.

Just like everything in life, meeting the right guy will more than likely take effort and patience. You'll have to put yourself out there and expose yourself to being found. You may have to do something that's outside your comfort zone. Don't waste precious time by just waiting for the man of your dreams. Put in some effort during the wait.

I had to step out of my comfort zone and ask Tod out for us to start dating, which was something I rarely did when I was single. I tell the story of how that happened in Chapter 13.

Finding a partner is a skillset we're not taught in school. If we don't learn it from our parents, how do we learn it? Trial and error. And then if we don't learn from each experience, we can be hard on ourselves and blame ourselves for our mistakes.

Now, in the digital age we live in, online dating is the most popular and convenient way to meet a date or potential spouse.

Online Dating Services

Online dating has become a major part of the single lifestyle. Online dating sites have become much more popular now than when I was dating, but I did dabble in two sites: Match and eHarmony.

Finding dates online can be time consuming and over-whelming. I've heard a lot of people say it's like a part-time job, and I have to say I agree from what little I experienced. The joke is you can get a sore thumb from all your swiping left and right on a certain dating app, and depending on how much you swipe, you can develop calluses!

Interesting Online Dating Statistics:[13]

- ♥ More than 5,000 dating sites and apps exist worldwide (approximately 2,500 of them in the U.S.).

- ♥ The first Sunday in January is the year's busiest time for these sites. (A new relationship must be on the top of a lot of New Year's resolution lists!)

- ♥ Singles like dating profiles with four or more photos.

- ♥ Millennials swipe for ten hours a week on average.

- ♥ Over 70 percent of online daters say lying on profiles is very common.

This proves you must be wise and discerning and not naive when getting to know someone.

First, I'd advise investing your time and energy only on dating sites that are in alignment with the type of relationship you want. Are you looking for a long-term relationship, i.e., marriage, or just a fun date?

Investigate the various sites before you jump in, then set up a profile on one that fits. Be honest, as the truth will come out sometime and you don't want to be exposed as a liar. After all, you want the other person to be honest as well.

Dating sites with video calls have become popular for singles seeking a low-risk way to meet new people. You can chat on video and get a fairly good idea if you want to move forward with an in-person date. You can also find out if they actually look like their profile photos!

Aside from dating apps, I've heard fun stories about people reconnecting with high school sweethearts on social media sites such as Facebook. Sometimes people reconnect who haven't spoken in twenty to thirty years!

While the internet is convenient and a lot of people do discover good dating possibilities online, others prefer to find dates in person. Following are a few of many options.

Restaurants, Bars, or Clubs

As I mentioned earlier, I was never enthusiastic about the bar scene. Rather than late-night bar hopping, I enjoyed an occasional happy hour after work. I could meet and chat with other professionals who were also unwinding and socializing for a few hours after the workday. I also liked going out for a dinner with friends.

I'm not saying that you can't or won't find the right guy in a bar or club, because of course it can happen. However, going to bars weekend after weekend can get old—or at least it did for me—so I found other options.

For happy hour or dinner, select restaurants that fit the type of guy you're seeking. If you're attracted to professional businessmen, go to a restaurant in a business district. If you're interested in meeting a laidback guy, go to a more casual, fun bar where people play pool or watch sports.

Meetup Groups

Many different Meetup groups are available, including singles groups. Some even specify certain age parameters or single parents. You can join a group that's involved with various activities you enjoy, such as dancing, traveling, running, skiing, snowboarding, reading, and much more. That way, even if you don't meet a love interest through a Meetup outing, at least you're out with other people spending time doing something you enjoy.

Other Possibilities for Finding Dates

You can also find love:

- ♥ **Through friends and colleagues.** A great (and probably the safest) way to meet dates is through friends, colleagues, and family members. I always preferred meeting dates through people I knew because they were likely to be somewhat familiar with the person and his background. Thus, I could learn a few things about the guy beforehand and wasn't going into a date completely blind.

- ♥ **At work.** Dating at work has become a little more complicated these days with dating policies, but depending on where you work and the company's specific policies, this may be a good place to meet someone. At least you have something in common.

- ♥ **At the gym.** Be approachable. Don't have your earbuds in the entire time you're there or

continuously have your head down looking at text
messages or social media. Look around, make eye
contact. That's a great way to connect.

- ♥ **At an airport or on an airplane.** I mention this
  because I actually met someone at an airport and
  was approached by someone on an airplane. We
  weren't sitting next to each other, but he had the
  flight attendant give me a note.

- ♥ **In your neighborhood or apartment complex.**
  A lot of apartment complexes hold tenant functions,
  or you could meet someone at the pool or out walking
  in the neighborhood. Get to know your neighbors
  and be friendly—not just for dating purposes, but
  to be neighborly.

- ♥ **At church.** Churches have various groups, and
  sometimes specifically singles groups. Tod and I are
  in a Life Group/Bible study with three other couples
  (but not all church groups are couples). I love the
  bond we have in our group and always know we can
  count on one another for support, advice, and prayer.
  As a single woman, even if you don't meet a potential
  partner, you can always benefit from that kind of
  support.

- ♥ **Look for opportunities every day.** You are
  surrounded by people every day at the gym,
  grocery store, coffee shop, public transportation,
  etc. All you need to do is open your eyes, quit

                                    Single K**NO**W More

looking at your phone, and show yourself to be friendly by smiling and saying Hi or striking up a conversation. I know of a woman who met her husband on a bus. He was the bus driver!

♥ **Through a matchmaker.** If you don't like to go to bars, you're not a social butterfly, or you're just super busy and don't have time to search yourself, a matchmaker could work out well. Although it will cost you something, you'll get one-on-one attention and a super-targeted approach.

Those are just a few ways you can get out and possibly meet someone to date—or just end up gaining new friends, which is a good thing in itself.

You never know when or where you're going to meet someone special. You just need to get out with a smile on your face and be approachable! As I mentioned earlier, love won't come knocking on your door. Even the guy who delivers packages rings the doorbell then hustles off these days.

Dating Safely

When you meet someone for a first date (whether it's someone you met online or offline), I highly recommend you keep it simple, such as meeting for coffee. This will make it much easier to cut the visit short in case you quickly realize you feel no connection or something didn't match up with the person's profile. Also, meet during the day where other people are gathered for safety purposes. You can never be too careful until you get to know someone and gain trust. Following is a story that illustrates what can happen and the kind of thing you want to avoid.

A Cautionary Tale

I heard about an educated seventy-one-year-old woman who went on a dating site and chose to date a seventy-five-year-old doctor. Safe, right? They met for coffee first, and things seemed to go well, so he invited her out to a fine restaurant for a second date. They were to meet at his house in an upscale neighborhood, and he would drive them to the restaurant from there. She wanted to see where he lived, so she agreed. He invited her in and offered her a snack because it would be a little while before they ate.

The snack happened to be a brownie laced with marijuana, but she wasn't made aware of that. She managed to get through the restaurant meal and collapsed when she got back to his house. He made advances that indicated he intended to take advantage of her condition. She described a "very scary trip." Her daughter texted her to ask how her date went. Fortunately, the woman was able to text her back to come and get her. Her daughter came and also called the police.

Although nothing physically disastrous happened to this woman, it well could have if this man had been forceful or intent on harm. As it was, the experience was traumatizing. She said, "Even though I wasn't physically harmed, I feel violated. I feel more vulnerable. The experience has eroded my sense of personal safety." Because she herself is trustworthy and kind, she trusted that other professionals would be as well. Not necessarily true.

So, ladies, don't assume someone can be trusted, no matter how old or how wealthy the person is or what his profession may be. Be acutely aware of red flags. Don't go to someone's house unless you know him well enough to know you're safe. Let someone know if you're going on a date with a new person you don't know, and arrange a check-in with them. One more bit of advice: Don't accept a brownie, no matter how much you like chocolate! Safety should always be at the top of your mind.

Safety Guidelines

Following are points to consider and actions you can take to be safe:

- ♥ Before you date someone, I suggest you use the internet to your advantage. I'm a firm believer in doing research on potential dates. Check out the guy's social media sites and Google search his name. A little background checking never hurts, especially if you feel something may be off. Your intuition is usually on target, so don't ignore it. For one thing, you can tell by an internet search if someone has ever been arrested.

  I admit, I checked out my husband online before our first date. In fact, I checked out everything I possibly could, including his hobbies, his social media sites, and the business he owned. I had every reason to be careful, as this was after my experience with Mark. Thankfully, all I found with Tod were *green* flags.

♥ **For your first several dates, meet your date at the location of the date.** Always meet where other people are gathered, not in isolated places. Coffee shops are great for first dates. Don't let dates pick you up from your home or meet them at theirs until you feel comfortable and know you can trust them. Don't just have a few online conversations and think you know or can trust someone and give the guy your home address.

♥ **Be aware of catfishing.** Catfishing refers to when a person takes information and images from other people and uses them to create a new identity for themselves. In other words, they pretend to be a different person than they are. Ways to tell if someone is catfishing you: They avoid video calls and face-to-face meetings, ask for money, ask for explicit (sexual) photos of you, use only professional photos to represent themselves. If something seems off, trust your instincts and do some research on how to identify a catfisher.

♥ **Dig deep and ask questions.** You know nothing or little about someone or their intentions at first. Don't be afraid to ask questions. Getting to know someone is an essential part of all relationships.

Reading body language and listening to voice tone are as important as the words that come out of someone's mouth. This is one reason for a video chat before dating someone.

♥ **Be careful when using Uber and Lyft for transportation** for late nights and after drinking alcohol. Always make sure you're getting in the correct car (even during the day). When ordering a car, you will be informed of the driver's name, license plate number, and vehicle description. Be sure the car you're getting into matches the car that's scheduled to pick you up. I've heard, and I'm sure you have as well, a few rideshare stories that ended in tragedy.

♥ **I highly recommend not drinking on a first date.** If you do have an alcoholic drink, have only one, and never leave your drink unattended, whether it's alcoholic or nonalcoholic. I've known women who've had their drinks spiked when they've left them unattended. This is another reason coffee dates are a good option for first dates, so alcohol isn't a temptation.

♥ **On a first date, always let a friend or family member know where you're going and with whom.** You can never be too safe. Trust your intuition if something doesn't feel right. Listen to your gut. Don't blow it off or feel silly. It's always best to be safe.

♥ **Take your phone and make sure it's fully charged when you leave on a date.** You never know when you'll need it.

Now we've covered where you might meet men to date and how to approach dating safely. Next, we'll address the part that timing plays in dating and what to do if you become involved in a relationship that doesn't work out. Unfortunately, that experience is common and it's wise to be aware of how to heal and move on if necessary.

Chapter 8

BREAKUPS HAPPEN – TIMING IS EVERYTHING

Sorry.
The person you are trying to reach
has moved on.
~ Anonymous

Life is all about timing. It's one of the many factors in relationships, and timing has played an important part in my life journey. I've learned to trust that everything happens when it's supposed to for my learning and growth, even though many times it doesn't seem like it!

Timing can make or break a relationship. Here's one of my breakup stories in which timing played a part.

I dated a guy who had two children. I'd never dated a guy with children, so this was a new experience for me. I wasn't sure what the relationship would entail. "John" had full custody of his seven-year-old daughter and nine-year-old son, both of whom rarely saw their mother. On the weekends, John was always tired and didn't want to do much. But I understood. He was a single parent busy with the kids, and he owned a business, so he spent a lot of time working. His plate was full. I had no children and a mediocre job at the time, so on the weekends, I didn't think about work and I had plenty of free time and energy. I didn't mind that we didn't do much. I enjoyed hanging out with him and his children. Usually, one weekend night the kids stayed with a babysitter and we had a "real" date night.

Every year John's entire family (mom, dad, three brothers, and their spouses and children) take a family trip. That year, I was invited to go with them to Sea Island Resort in Georgia. The resort was gorgeous, and we were there over the Fourth of July. Our room had two queen beds. I shared a bed with his daughter, and he shared a bed with his son. Not the most romantic vacation, but it was a family vacation, so it was totally fine and the appropriate thing to do. But it wasn't exactly how I had envisioned our first vacation together.

When just the two of us got some pockets of free time, he wanted to nap—but not me! We were on vacation at a beautiful resort! I wanted to explore all that the resort had to offer and enjoy our alone time together. We ended up getting into a little tiff during the vacation, which spiraled into a full-blown argument, and we barely talked the last few days on vacation. Shortly after the trip, we broke up.

John's life was full as a single dad taking care of his children full time and running a business. On the other hand, I was ready to focus 100 percent on this relationship, but I was getting only about 50 percent of his focus and effort in return. We just weren't on the same page. It wasn't an easy breakup, and being close to his family and children made it extra emotional. I not only felt the emptiness of not having him in my life anymore, but I felt the emptiness of not seeing his children and family. Sometimes breaking up with the family is just as hard as breaking up with the guy.

As difficult as some of my breakups were, I thank God that all of those relationships didn't work out and I didn't settle because I wouldn't be where I am today, married to a wonderful man.

When I met Tod, I knew what I was looking for in a relationship and future husband, and I wasn't willing to settle for less. This accounts for why I was single for fifteen years after my first marriage.

I don't think I would have appreciated my husband's awesome qualities if I'd have met him sooner, so the timing was perfect. Yes, we would have had the opportunity to spend more years together, but I don't know if I would have married him years earlier. I was in a different place, a different season. I needed to experience my journey before meeting him to know what was important to me in a relationship, what wasn't important, and what I needed in my forever love.

Like most things in life, dating is a learning experience, and with each relationship or date, we learn something—good, bad, or both. It's those experiences that help get us get to where we want to be.

When I was in my twenties, I experienced a lot of life changes, a lot of seasons. I was maturing—figuring out what career direction I wanted to pursue and where I wanted to live, learning how to manage finances and be independent. I was in the midst of major learning experiences.

Timing played a part in my decision to move from Las Vegas to Newport Beach. The move was a little scary but a lot exciting. I had lived in Las Vegas for twenty years, so the idea of moving was a big decision. I didn't have to move; I had a great job and wonderful friends, I owned a home, and I was comfortable, but I knew I was ready for a change.

I made a deal with myself: I would put my house on the market and if my house sold, I would move to California. I was in no rush; it was just an idea.

Well, I put my house on the market and it sold within a week. The buyer paid cash, and I had thirty days to move out! I thought, *Okay, this is meant to happen,* so I packed up my house and moved on to a new chapter in my life.

You might be wondering why I chose Newport Beach. Other than it being one of the most beautiful places in the United States, my sister lives there. When I visited her, I fell in love with the beauty, the weather, and the beach lifestyle. I refer to it as a little slice of heaven.

I thought for sure when I moved there that the dating pool would be better. I soon found out that was not the case. As it turned out, Newport Beach had a smaller, more fickle dating pool than Las Vegas. I've concluded that no matter where one lives, there will always be negatives and positives when it comes to dating.

However, I never gave up on knowing that good men were out there. I never gave up on love. I bet you've heard one of your friends say that *all the good men are taken.* Not true. How can all the good guys be taken? Ladies, there are still good men out there. Be patient, stay positive, show up friendly, and when the time is right and the right person comes along, the magic and connection will happen. Trust the process; trust God's timing. In the meantime, be prepared for breakups.

Healing from Breakups

If you break up with someone, congratulations for getting out of a relationship that wasn't working   even if the breakup wasn't intentional on your part. Take what you learned with you into the next chapter of your life and don't give up.

Breakups are okay, starting over is okay, being alone is okay. What's not okay is staying in a relationship where you're not respected, not loved, abused, or unhappy.

Whether you end the relationship or your partner ends it, breakups are painful, and you need to go through a healing process. It's torture to not forgive yourself and not move on from past experiences. Don't get caught in the prison of your past and let your past relationships hold you back from pursuing what you deserve and crave. Learn from mistakes and move on.

Dealing with breakup aftermath can feel like picking up the pieces after an explosion of emotions. Oh yes, I know how those emotional explosions feel. I've been there myself—a few times. I learned not to get caught up and stuck in all the emotions, but to acknowledge them and then move through them.

Write About How You Feel

For me, writing about how I feel helps me release my feelings and emotions.

I recommend you write down your thoughts in a journal. Write about how you're feeling or write a letter to your ex—but don't send it. You are simply venting. It will help you release pent-up emotions and get clear.

Life and time are too precious to spend dwelling at length on the past and a relationship that didn't work out. Switch your mentality from *I'm broken and sad* to *I'm growing and healing.* Healing is a journey, one day at a time. You will have bad days and maybe some horrible days, but you'll also have good days. I like the saying, "Fall down seven times, stand up eight." This is true with everything in life. If you fall down, get back up! Each time you get back up, you will be wiser and stronger.

     Single KNOW More

Allow Time for Detox

Don't jump into another relationship too quickly! Allow time for a breakup detox.

When I had a breakup, I would set a certain amount of time to let all my feelings and emotions come out (sad, mad, lonely). This not only helped me mentally, but it helped heal me and prepare me for my next relationship down the road. My timeline for detox depended on my level of involvement in the relationship that just ended. I recommend that approach. It's cleansing.

A great way to release stress and frustration is by going to the gym and working out and sweating! It may be a struggle to get to the gym or go outside for a walk or jog, but when you've finished working out, you'll be so glad you did. Exercising and sweating help release feel-good endorphins and get you out of a funk!

I've never said after a workout, "I wish I hadn't done that."

Find Support

Get together with friends and family. Doing this will help keep your mind occupied and it feels good to share feelings with others. Hugging, laughing, human connection, and encouragement are great healers. Talk to people who will give you positive advice and make you feel good, not jaded or negative people who love to see others go through tough times to make themselves feel better. The people you surround yourself with are so important. Make sure they are loving and positive.

Focus on You

After a breakup is a great time to focus on *you*. Reevaluate your life. Maybe your needs and goals have shifted a little—or a lot! This is a good time to assess your life and make adjustments or improvements.

Press the dating Pause button. It's very important and healthy to know how to be happy and feel whole being alone and loving yourself. Use this delicate time to work on yourself, to work on a healthy foundation. Some women don't feel validated without a man in their life. They feel they always have to be in a relationship, and consequently, they have no time to themselves. Some don't want to go through the pain of healing from a breakup, so they go from relationship to relationship to mask the hurt. But that doesn't help.

Slow down. After a breakup, give yourself time to process alone. Otherwise, it isn't fair to the next man if you carry emotional baggage into the following relationship. This also applies to men. Beware if you meet a man who just got out of a long-term relationship. He may not be ready to jump into another relationship. Men are just as guilty as women of jumping from relationship to relationship.

Don't Be a Stalker

Stalking of an ex has *desperate* written all over it. Save yourself the heartbreak and possible embarrassment. After a breakup:

- ♥ Don't stalk your ex's every move on social media and try to figure out if he's dating someone.

- ♥ Don't show up at places where you know he likes to hang out and hope you'll run into him.

- ♥ Don't call or text him after having a few cocktails or, worse yet, when you're drunk.

- ♥ Don't drive by his place at 2 a.m. and look for strange cars parked at his house.

Doing any of this will slow down your healing process. Invest your time and energy in more productive ways that will benefit you and your future.

Befriend—or Seek Revenge?

If you go on one or two dates with someone and know right away the relationship isn't going anywhere but the two of you have a lot in common, perhaps you've just met a new friend.

If a relationship ends mutually, it's possible you can remain friends. But in reality how many relationships end mutually? Usually one of you hopes that being friends might lead to you getting back together.

Personally, I didn't end up being friends with anyone after dating them. Sometimes we had a cordial relationship, but we weren't what I would consider friends.

If the relationship doesn't end cordially, don't plot revenge against an ex. It's a waste of time and energy, and it creates stress.

Some people put more effort into breakup revenge than they put into the relationship! It seems that when you suddenly don't have something you enjoyed, focusing on it becomes a priority. However, the best revenge is working on you and your health. *Water the flowers in your life, not the weeds.*

When the Breakup Involves More Than Two People

If the person you're breaking up with has children you spent time with, got to know and love, and became part of your life, it's even more difficult ending that relationship. I know because I experienced it.

If the two of you have pets together, who gets custody of the dog or cat when you split up? This one I didn't experience, but I imagine it would also be a painful situation. A breakup is emotionally difficult in itself, and when you throw in these other variables, the pain can be magnified. It's even more important to follow the suggested healing guidelines.

When the Breakup Involves Your Living Space

I was dating a guy for about a year and our relationship was moving along great. Then, out of nowhere, he was informed he had to relocate to San Francisco for his job. He owned a home in Orange County and he didn't want to sell it. His plan was to keep that home and rent it, and move into a rental in San Francisco.

He wasn't thrilled about renting his home, but his choices were to either rent or sell it. It so happened, my lease was up on my apartment, so we decided I would move into his house and rent it. This sounded like an awesome decision that would benefit both of us. I would have a nice house to live in and he wouldn't have to rent to a stranger. In addition, he would be able to come back to Orange County every weekend and stay in his house with me. It was a great plan.

Well, you know what they say about "best laid plans." After I moved in, he ended up not having to move to San Francisco, and because I had already moved in, we decided to live together. I had never lived with anyone, but I was comfortable with this decision. Everything ended up working out well and life was great—until we split up eight months later.

Ending our relationship was heartbreaking, and I had no idea where I was going to live. Just like that, my life completely changed. I was no longer in a relationship, and I had to figure out where my next home would be after just getting settled into where I was living.

Thank goodness my sister lived in a large home and had a guest room I could move into temporarily until I figured out where my new home would be. I lived with my sister for about three months and then moved into my own beautiful place. I was ready for a fresh start—a new season in my life.

I have three points for you to consider if you're thinking about moving in with someone:

♥ If marriage is your goal, how much is living together going to prolong getting married? Is living together something you want to do to see if the two of you would be compatible for marriage? If so, discuss this with your partner. Perhaps set a timeframe in which to decide your compatibility. He may not want to get married. Let him know where you stand.

- ♥ If you break up, just know that one of you will have to move out of that cozy home you live in together. In my case, my ex owned the home, so obviously I was the one who had to pack up and move. Given your financial arrangements, maybe both of you will have to move. Be mentally prepared for that possibility.

- ♥ If a guy moves into *your* home, make sure he pays his portion of the mortgage or rent and other expenses. A freeloader is a red flag.

When I see someone struggling after a breakup, I can relate. "Heartbreak Hotel" is a miserable place to be in, and it just sucks. It can generate gut-wrenching, horrible feelings. When ending a long-term relationship with a lot of history, it takes time to heal and get back to a routine that doesn't involve your ex. You no longer have that person who was part of your life every single day, your best friend.

You obviously broke up for a reason that couldn't be resolved. Either both of you agreed to end the relationship, or it was one-sided. Whatever the reason, the relationship was not meant to be. If it was the other person's decision, you have to respect the way he feels. At least he's being honest with you and not leading you on or staying in the relationship and lying or cheating.

You just have to move through the changes, and one day you will have joy back in your life.

   Single KNOW More

Look for the Rainbow

As hard as breakups can be, the end game can be a blessing. I had some really tough breakups, and a few times, I wondered how I could ever be happy again. Yet here I am today, thankful for all of my breakups and glad those relationships didn't work out. Why? Now I see clearly that they were flawed, and I am right where I should be.

Today, we tend to want everything to be easy and quick. But there's no Easy button for heartbreak recovery. We just need to know we can handle almost everything, even if it takes time. God has equipped us to deal with difficult situations.

It helps to know that things happen for a reason and to expect a rainbow after the storm. For sure, that's easier said than done. In the midst of heartbreak, it's super tough to even think or to imagine you will ever be happy again. However, if you keep a positive mindset, it will help a lot! Again, learn what you can from your experiences, grow from them, and don't give up.

If I had stayed with any of the men I dated long term, I wouldn't have ended up with the awesome husband I have today. That makes all my breakups worthwhile.

I hope you have gained a healthy perspective and helpful hints from this chapter on timing and breakups. Ideally, this knowledge will also help you to build self-confidence, which is the topic of Chapter 9.

HOW AND WHY TO HAVE SELF-CONFIDENCE

Self-confidence is a super power.
Once you start to believe in yourself,
magic starts happening.
~ Anonymous

Self-confidence is critical to both attracting a good man and having a healthy relationship. Have you heard of the Law of Attraction? You attract what you think about and believe. Therefore, the more you talk about bad dates, believe all the good men are taken, or think you don't deserve a great guy, the more you'll continue to have bad dates and not find a good man.

The way to attract someone who respects and loves you is first to respect and love yourself. Then, always think positively about what you *want* and *not* what you *don't* want.

Picture yourself with the man of your dreams, envision him as if he is already in your life. Envision what he looks like from head to toe. Picture your dream vacation with him and how well he treats you. Write out specifically what you want in a man and what's important to you in a relationship. Have the self-confidence to believe you can have what you want. Don't give up.

I'll tell you how that particular piece of advice became important to me.

Don't Be a Quitter

Something happened in junior high school that left a lasting impression on me. I remember it whenever I think about quitting or giving up on something.

I was athletic growing up. I played softball, basketball, and volleyball, and I ran track. I decided I wanted to quit basketball in eighth grade. I can't remember exactly why I wanted to quit, but I remember to this day what the coach said to me when I told her that's what I wanted to do. She looked me in the eye and said, "Joyce, if you quit, you will be a quitter the rest of your life." Whoa! That bold statement has stuck with me. Every time I think about quitting something, I remember those words from my basketball coach in eighth grade, and it has turned me around a few times when I wanted to quit.

Thank you, eighth-grade basketball coach! Oh, and by the way, I didn't quit the basketball team. I continued playing throughout my senior year in high school.

Why Is Self-Confidence So Important?

I think we can all agree, confidence is attractive. We admire people who are self-confident. It's not about being arrogant or being the best. True confidence is calm and quiet. Unfortunately, however, having self-confidence is a struggle for many people. A hidden fear in most of us arises from lack of confidence.

Being confident in a relationship is a must and can be one of your greatest assets. Self-confidence is having genuinely positive feelings about yourself while accepting your faults. This means that even when you don't like things about yourself, you love your whole self, and you aren't embarrassed or held back by your faults.

Self-confidence is a mindset of accepting and trusting yourself and believing in your ability to handle life. Sounds simple, right? Simple but not easy, or everyone would be confident.

I consider myself a confident woman, but I've had to build confidence over the years. Like most of us, I'm a work in progress. What I've gone through personally and profession-ally and what I've learned from my victories and defeats have helped build my confidence foundation.

When I was single, I lived by myself. I managed my finances, negotiated and purchased cars by myself, purchased a home at thirty-four years old, sold two homes, and even fixed my toilet! I did a lot on my own, and sometimes the load was quite heavy doing everything by myself. Looking back now, though, I'm grateful I experienced all of it. The ups and downs and stretching myself helped expand my knowledge and make me stronger, wiser, and more confident.

I accomplished a lot on my own, and I didn't *need* a man. I was capable of living by myself. The thing is, I *wanted* a man in my life; I wanted a partner. I proved I could live on my own, but I preferred to do life with a partner—and I think I'm not the only woman to feel that way! The thing is, it's disempowering to come from need. A man likes to think he's an asset, of course, but he probably doesn't want the heavy responsibility of being a total *necessity.*

Confidence Balance in a Relationship

When Tod and I got married, Tod began helping out with the heavy load I was used to taking on myself. I admit it felt really good! For example, Tod loves to drive and he's a great driver—maybe a little too aggressive and fast sometimes, but good. He's the best parallel parker I have ever seen. While I don't mind driving, I prefer being the passenger and being chauffeured around. I found myself not driving very often. However, when I *did* drive, I felt I was losing my driving

                                    Single KNOW More

skills a little. I was driving slower and more cautiously, and I wasn't confident parking in tight spaces. This made me quickly realize my confidence when driving had slipped a little and I needed to drive more and not always be the passenger.

It's great having a partner to help out, but I also want to keep up on all my skills and feel confident. I want to be sharp and continue to grow, not become stagnant because someone is doing a lot for me.

My husband is also a fixer. Anytime I can't figure something out or something isn't going right and I tell him about it, he jumps right in and wants to fix it. Most of the time, I greatly appreciate his eagerness to solve problems, but if I want to fix something on my own, I know I have to approach it differently and just ask for his advice, not help.

Bottom line? It's awesome having a partner to help out, because we all have so much going on, but make sure you don't lose your confidence or your skills. Maintain a healthy balance so you stay sharp and confident in all areas.

Your Appearance and Self-Confidence

When you feel good about your appearance, doesn't it boost your self-confidence? And vice versa: When you feel like you don't look your best, it's likely to diminish your self-confidence and affect the way you carry yourself and interact with people.

Take a shower, wash and style your hair, and put on a little makeup and an attractive outfit. Look sharp and put together! I know when I occasionally go out to run a quick errand to the post office or grocery store with no makeup, wearing sweats and a cap, I hope I don't run into anyone I know. And if I do,

I feel uncomfortable and kick myself in the butt about how I look.

When you know you look good, it shows. You have a little more bounce in your step and you feel good. When you *feel* like your best self, you're more able to *be* your best self. What makes *you* feel like your best self?

For me, other than looking put together, I feel my best when I'm eating healthy, at my goal weight, hanging out with family and friends, and making people feel happy and good.

My husband jokes with me about how happy I get on days I have a hair appointment. I confess it is a happy day. After my appointment, my hair color is fresh and my hair is styled perfectly, and I feel great! I swear it immediately takes a few years off!

Before I was an entrepreneur, I worked eight-to-five jobs. I showered every morning, washed and styled my hair, dressed in nice clothes, and arrived at work by 8 a.m. Now that I am an entrepreneur and I'm my own boss, some days when I work from our home office, I wear my yoga pants and slippers all day, with no makeup and my hair in a ponytail. Yes, it's pretty awesome I get to do that if I want, but after doing relaxed mode for a day or two, it feels good to step it up.

As much as I love having days I don't have to dress up for anyone, I know when I'm dressed nicely and well put together, I feel more attractive and confident, and sometimes more productive.

When you're dating and getting to know a new man, of course you want to look your best. However, it's also important to let him see the "real" you early in the relationship. Let him

 Single KNOW More

see the beautiful imperfect you! Not you hiding behind layers of makeup and lash and hair extensions.

A friend of mine who's a makeup artist told me about a lady who's married to a plastic surgeon and always feels like she must look perfect. She has a makeup artist and hairdresser come to her house every morning to get her beautified for the day so her husband sees her looking like a perfect Barbie doll.

This approach sounds *way* too stressful to me. I want my husband to love me all the time, not just when I'm all dolled up. Luckily, Tod tells me I'm beautiful even when I wake up in the morning as natural as it gets.

Embrace your natural beauty and don't be intimidated or afraid to be you. Be confident in your real skin!

A beautiful thing to wear that will not only boost your mood and confidence but make you more attractive is a *smile*. Smiling costs nothing, is usually effortless, and can make a *big* impact on yourself and others around you. When you smile, people will smile more at you.

"Science has shown that the mere act of smiling can lift your mood, lower stress, boost your immune system, and possibly even prolong your life."[14]

Not only is smiling beneficial for you, but you could make someone's day by smiling at them and showing them you're friendly. You have a lot more power than you know to make someone's day. You never know what people are going through.

Plus, smiling will make you more friendly looking and approachable, which means you'll be more attractive to men.

Don't you think someone is more attractive when smiling? I do.

Positive Affirmations for Self-Confidence

Another way to boost self-confidence is to think positively about yourself as much as possible. Remind yourself daily that you are a unique, special, valuable person, and you deserve to be happy and feel good about yourself.

I keep an affirmation on my computer that I see and feed my mind with *every day.* It reads: I AM . . . and each day I fill in the blank:

- ♥ I AM beautiful.
- ♥ I AM worthy.
- ♥ I AM healthy.
- ♥ I AM strong.
- ♥ I AM confident.

Sometimes negative thoughts enter my mind such as:

- ♥ I can't do this.
- ♥ I'm not pretty.
- ♥ I need to lose weight.

When these pop up, I immediately change them to positive affirmations. I don't want any negative thoughts to affect my actions, mindset, and mood, so I keep my thinking positive!

Post *your* affirmations where you see them daily: on your computer, refrigerator, bathroom mirror, nightstand, or in your car. Eliminate the words *I can't* and *I'm not* from your vocabulary and thoughts.

You'll see your life begin to reflect your more positive mindset and outlook.

Possible Negative Effects of Social Media

Social media can be a big confidence crusher. It gives the impression that some people are close to perfect and portrays unrealistic goals—so I advise you to limit your time on these sites.

On social media, you see people (most of whom you don't even know personally) posting beautiful photos of traveling, their beautiful home and children, and so on. This can make you feel your life isn't good enough or you're not this enough or that enough.

Keep in mind that what you're seeing on social media isn't always reality. Many people can be feeling miserable behind their smiles, filters, and failing relationships. Very few people expose their imperfect, unfiltered life on social media. Therefore, don't become envious and let their so-called perfect life get you down. Keep focused on *your* life and what is important to *you*.

I admit that sometimes what I see on social media makes me feel as if my life is falling short; but most of the time, I use it to fuel my abilities to do better and get what *I* want. I put it all into perspective and realize I have many blessings they may not.

Always be mindful that what you post online reflects you and what you want to attract. So (let's say) most of your posts on social media are sexy selfies with a cocktail in hand. Guess what! You'll attract a certain kind of attention from a certain kind of man. And that's fine if that's what you intend and desire.

I'm not saying you should just post photos of you baking apple pie and wearing turtlenecks. However, consider the type of man you want to attract and post accordingly—but post honestly. Reflect your real life.

Fear, the Self-Confidence Showstopper

Fear is one of the most crippling things we deal with in life. It can hold us back from making decisions and reaching our goals, make us avoid what we need to confront, and destroy our self-confidence.

Don't let fear cheat you out of what you'd like to have or achieve. You don't want to look back in five or ten years and be upset that you didn't chase a dream or desire.

Have you ever let fear control you and hold you back from doing something? My guess is you said yes because fear is something that *all* of us experience. Your mind can stop you in your tracks and make you think you're not good enough or that something bad will happen if you step out of your comfort zone.

My Fear of Writing This Book

When my husband and I first started talking about the idea of me writing this book, I loved the idea. I got excited and immediately had many thoughts about what I wanted to share in the book. But then fear got to me. With my personality type, I rarely put myself out there and don't like to be in the spotlight. So opening myself up and writing *Single KNOW More* aroused a roller coaster of emotions. One day I'd be on a high and excited, and the next I'd hear voices in my head trying to pull me down:

> *Joyce, you can't do this.*
> *What if it's a miserable failure?*
> *Why would anyone take YOUR advice?*
> *You're just going to embarrass yourself!*
> **UGH!!!**

Nearly every day, I had to push past negative thoughts in my head and turn the channel to a positive thought.

Some days I thought I couldn't do it; other days I thought it was the best idea ever! But I wanted to write this book, and I knew I could do it. I wasn't going to let other people's opinions or, most of all, my own negative thoughts or insecurity stop me. It's too exhausting wondering what other people think. Obviously my desire won over fear because you're reading my book!

I won't be looking back saying *What if* … I've had too many What ifs in my life because of fear. I'm stronger than *What ifs* and so are *you!*

Standing Up to Fear

It takes courage to stand up and face your fears because fear is built into the human system. It's always going to be in your life. The best way to defeat fear is to resist it right when it enters your mind.

Fear shows up in many ways, such as:

- ♥ doubt,

- ♥ insecurity,

- ♥ worry,

- ♥ anxiety, and

- ♥ panic.

Fear kills ambition and prevents joy. It keeps us from moving forward toward our dreams.

The Bible includes many statements such as "Fear not" and "Be not afraid," so God certainly doesn't want us to be fearful![15]

We're consuming so much fear these days that it's taking a toll on many people and creating panic. If you have children, try not to show your fearfulness in front of them. They feel, hear, and see what you model. If you are living in fear, they will feel your energy and be fearful as well. Instead, be an example of strength and courage. Teach them reasonable discretion where needed, of course, but teach them to be fearless.

You can run from fear—it's easy and anyone can do it—or you can tackle it with courage—which not a lot of people do because it's scary and uncomfortable. However, the more you challenge yourself and expose yourself to uncomfortable situations, the more courage and mental strength you gain. *Life doesn't get easier, baby, but you get tougher.*

Find ways to challenge yourself and your fears daily. This can look like any of the following:

- ♥ Learning to fix things around the house
- ♥ Learning how to handle your finances
- ♥ Expanding your knowledge by taking a class
- ♥ Creating something to sell or show
- ♥ Using your talents in a bigger way
- ♥ Speaking in public
- ♥ Taking trips by yourself
- ♥ Possibly moving to another place
- ♥ Going out more to meet eligible men
- ♥ Asking a guy out

While you may meet with less than success at times, you'll be adding to your repertoire of experiences, wisdom, knowledge, and skills. If you're not a quitter and you don't give up, you'll find yourself getting stronger, and your self-confidence will soar. This can only improve your life!

Another thing that can improve your life is learning how to communicate effectively, the very subject of the next chapter.

Chapter 10

HONEST COMMUNICATION – THE KEY TO ALL HEALTHY RELATIONSHIPS

*The biggest communication problem
is we don't listen to understand.
We listen to reply.*
~ Anonymous

Yes, communication is a critical factor in all relationships, and it's in danger of losing its human connection with the rise of technology. Where's the eye contact? Where are the nuances of emotion and meaning? Where's the deep conversation? This chapter looks at the various aspects of communication that are so integral to a meaningful relationship.

Listening

Let's start with one of the most important and endangered communication skills—*listening.* Learning to carefully (fully with care) listen may be as difficult as learning a foreign language. It takes effort and skill. We make listening more problematic than it has to be because we're often thinking about how we're going to respond. This can distract us from fully listening to the person speaking. If we make a conscious effort to *listen,* we might be amazed at what we learn and the deeper connections we can make.

"Research has indicated that the average person listens for only seventeen seconds before interrupting and interjecting their own ideas."[16] Conscious listening is something I work on continuously.

The Dangers of Digital Communication

In this digital age, face-to-face communication is increasingly on the decline. Technology can be more time-efficient and easier, but it detracts from building deep personal relationships. Have you ever received a text message or email and thought it meant one thing and then found out it meant something totally different?

Single KNOW More

When text messages and emails are taken out of context, it can create problems and sometimes leave us feeling confused or even hurt. When we have face-to-face communication, we get to experience real-time conversation, voice tone, and body language, which helps us fully understand what someone is communicating.

It's hard to believe people now end relationships over text and email. Even worse than breaking up that way is ghosting, or just disappearing with no explanation. If a guy has ghosted you or is currently ghosting you, it's a sign you should move on, because his true flakey character is showing. Ghosting is naturally easier to do if a relationship is largely digital—and ghosting in any form is an obvious red flag.

For some, technology is their best friend. Millennials and Gen Zers have been raised using technology. This makes face-to-face communication uncomfortable and harder for them, so they avoid it.

I love technology for its many benefits, but it's alarming to see how technology is affecting our overall well-being in such a negative way.

It's a sad fact that a lot of people would prefer looking down at their phone instead of into someone's eyes and having face-to-face conversation. Consider these statistics:[17]

♥ "Eighty-five percent of smartphone users check their phones while speaking with friends and family.

♥ We tap, swipe and click our phones 2,617 times per day.

- ♥ Seventy-three percent of us have experienced anxiety over losing our phones.

- ♥ Sixty percent of college students say they are addicted to their phones."

Technology is here to stay. I just hope it doesn't turn us into a bunch of emotionless robots with health issues.

Finding Balance in Use of Technology

To be healthy and happy, we need to create a balance between technology and the human connection. Adults and teens may have to readjust and retrain themselves. However, parents can teach their young children to develop good habits and a healthy balance with technology. Using technology may keep them busy and quiet, but other activities can accomplish this with a little creativity and thoughtfulness.

If you're a parent, teaching your children this balance will hopefully help you be more mindful with your own technology usage. It's not only healthy for *you*, but you can serve as a role model for your kids.

I've become more aware of my personal technology habits. I used to grab my phone every morning and skim through news headlines, Facebook, Instagram, email, and the weather. When I did this, I got pulled in many different directions, and most of the time, they weren't positive. Not a good way to start the day.

This led me to change my morning routine. Instead of grabbing my phone or watching the news, I drink my morning coffee and read at least four to five pages of a book or write in my gratitude journal. This sets the tone for my day, and I don't feel anxious from looking at my phone and reading stress-inducing news headlines.

Tips for Communicating Effectively

Consider the following suggestions for communicating so you have the clearest understanding and best connection with others.

Communicate live and direct. Whenever possible, it's more effective to communicate via phone and in-person conversations than by text or email. This is *especially* true when resolving a disagreement or talking about something important. As mentioned previously, it's much harder to communicate feelings and thoughts digitally, and words can get misinterpreted through technology.

Be honest. Communicating in a healthy relationship can sometimes mean talking about things you've never in your life talked about with another human being. Open yourself up to the full potential that a relationship can be. Communicate what you want—which is something I have learned to do.

Tod and I talk about everything, including things I never dreamed I would talk about with him or anyone else. I know when I talk to Tod, I can be vulnerable and he won't judge or criticize me.

In the beginning of our relationship, some of our conversations were uncomfortable for me. I'd never talked about certain things, especially with a guy, and I'm naturally a little closed up. However, because of the deep connection and real communication Tod and I have, we've grown together. We have a level of comfort and trust that didn't develop overnight but has developed with expressing our real feelings and having open honest communication.

Tod and I are always focusing and working on our relationship. When we hit bumps in the road and don't see eye to eye, we can resolve our differences quickly and not clam up or say things we'll regret. I used to run away from conflict, and now I face it—which pays off in the end.

If relationships are important to you, work on them continually.

Talk to people. This can be challenging for certain personality types who aren't very outgoing or social. When I was single, if I saw a guy at the gym or in a coffee shop and we had a little eye contact going, I normally didn't take it any further. I couldn't bring myself to simply strike up a conversation. Later I'd regret not being a little more assertive and was left wondering *what if* … because I'd probably never see that person again. Over time, I learned to be more approachable and a little more assertive with my approach.

Case in point: I was the one who made the first move and asked Tod if he would be interested in meeting for coffee or dinner. (See my full love story in Chapter 12). He had no idea I was even attracted to him. Although making the first move was something I rarely did when I was single, breaking out of my comfort zone worked out perfectly in this case!

Have you ever turned away from someone's gaze and looked down at your phone when you could have connected? Put your phone away and open yourself up. Be aware of who is around you. Think about what opportunities you may miss personally and professionally by having your head down and not paying attention.

We can all benefit from living in the moment a little more. Yesterday is gone and tomorrow is not guaranteed, so live each day in the moment.

Fully engage. When you're on a date, put your phone away and focus your attention on that person. Look him in the eye when talking, ask questions, and listen to get to know him.

I think we've all noticed couples, friends, or families sitting together in a restaurant who are more interested in checking their phones than looking at the person across the table and having a real conversation.

If you know someone only on the surface, what will happen when times get tough or difficult conversations arise? All you'll have is surface feelings and a surface understanding of the other person. You're going to become frustrated, stressed, and angry not knowing how to communicate and resolve issues.

Learn to communicate during stress and conflicts. Tod came into our relationship with awesome communication skills because he's been teaching these skills for decades. Although my own communication skills were okay, I didn't realize how poorly I communicated during conflict. I held things inside. When Tod and I first started dating and we had a disagreement, I would typically shut down. I'd run away and not want to talk, hoping the disagreement would just go away. How healthy is that? Not healthy at all. I kept those feelings festering inside.

Now I don't run away when things get uncomfortable. Tod and I talk about *everything*. This not only helps strengthen our marriage, but we don't hold on to issues that make us angry or hurt us. If we hung on to those painful feelings, they would continue to grow.

During conflict, if you tend to get defensive, withdraw, become angry, or just run for the hills and hope everything will magically be resolved, your behavior is likely being driven by hurt or fear. These feelings and reactions can block love and affection. Open up and talk about your feelings. Release any toxic thoughts or behavior. You can't have a healthy relationship if you're toxic.

When something triggers me, I usually want to react quickly. My heart starts racing and I feel anxious. My immediate reaction is typically not my best reaction. I know this from past experiences. So when I feel my heart start beating hard and fast, almost as if it's going to explode from my chest, I *stop*. I take a few deep breaths and think about how I really *want* to respond. I give myself time to calm down so I don't overreact. I don't want my tongue to beat my mind to the draw.

Relationships are constantly evolving, so it's important to keep communication open and verbalize your wants and needs, because those also change. If you don't *express* your wants and needs, you will be the only one who knows how you truly feel.

Be aware of how your communication style is being reflected back to you. Have you ever noticed that when you spend a lot of time with someone or watch someone on TV

Single KNOW More

a lot, you start to say certain things they say or mimic their body language or voice tone?

Tod and I spend *a lot* of time together, considering we're married and also work together, so we naturally pick up habits and mannerisms from each other. When I noticed this was happening, it was a big eye opener. Tod started unintentionally doing certain things I do or saying things I often say, and I didn't like some of it! Sometimes it came off as obnoxious or even rude. The eye opener was that I was saying and doing the same things and thought it was okay! Realizing this has definitely made me want to become a better role model and positive example. It makes me think of the saying *Treat others the way you want to be treated.* I've become more conscious of what I say and do to reflect how I want to be talked to and treated.

My experience is a true-life example of how we pick up habits from the people we hang out with the most. This makes sense because habits are formed through repetition, so we can unknowingly pick up habits from the people with whom we spend the most time.

Think about the person or people you spend the most time with and what habits you might be picking up from them. Just as you can absorb the bad habits and attitudes of the wrong crowd, you can acquire the good traits of the right crowd of happy, self-confident, motivating, and optimistic people. Consider this the next time you find yourself spending time with people who are unhappy, pessimistic, and unsuccessful. What habits would you rather adopt?

Being aware of your actions and words is also highly important if you have children. They're like sponges and pick up on a lot more than you may think. You are their role model. Show them a way to communicate respectfully and live positively and successfully. In a lot of ways, the world has become very different and difficult to navigate. Your children need you to teach them right from wrong. From the moment you first hold them in your arms and during their first crucial years, you are all they have. Your children look up to you and depend on you. Be aware of what you're teaching them by example, and be a kind, thoughtful, positive role model in *all* of your relationships.

Another common expression is *You teach people how to treat you.* This is especially relevant when it comes to dating and marriage. If someone isn't treating you respectfully, you need to let them know that's not acceptable. They will take cues from how you treat yourself, so once again, go back and read Chapter 1!

The next chapter addresses four basic personality types to help you understand how and why people act and communicate the way they do. Understanding promotes acceptance if someone has a different personality type than you do—and acceptance is necessary for healthy relationships.

Chapter 11

PERSONALITY AND COMMUNICATION STYLES

*In a relationship, when communication
starts to fade, everything else follows.
~ Unknown*

'm super excited to tell you about this topic, because once you know about different personality and communication styles, it will benefit all areas of your life, dating included!

We are all the same, but very different. Have you heard that saying? It's soooo true!

For decades, Tod has been teaching clients, friends, and family how to determine and communicate with different personality styles. Before I met Tod, I didn't realize there was such a thing, and now that I'm aware of these differences, it's been helpful in all my relationships. I've witnessed firsthand how knowing personality styles has been life-changing for people of all ages.

Tod and I are opposite personality styles, and knowing this helps us better understand and be more aware of each other's intentions and actions. It doesn't make our relationship perfect, of course, but it helps us quickly navigate through disagreements, decisions, and challenges we face.

It's almost impossible to change someone's personality, as much of our personality is formed within the first few years of our lives. Part of our personality is genetic, so we're born with it. The rest is formed through environmental influences and how we are raised. However, siblings can have quite different personalities, so many factors are involved.

We are all unique individuals, and one personality style is not better than another. All personalities have strengths and weaknesses. Just because someone doesn't act, dress, or talk the way you think they should, doesn't mean they're inferior or superior to anyone else.

Part of loving someone unconditionally is letting them be themselves even if you would do things differently. This doesn't mean you have to accept destructive or disrespectful behavior, however. You can choose to be with people with whom you're compatible. Let's look at these personality styles to give you a better understanding.

Four Basic Personality Styles

Many tools and techniques are available for learning personality styles, but all are based on four personality traits, in this case characterized by four different birds. Why birds? Well, the four bird types are easy to visualize and remember, and they're *fun.* I don't know about you, but when I'm learning something, *easy* and *fun* are always pluses for me!

Learning personality styles will not only help you understand what types of guys you're dating or want to date, but you'll also learn your own personality/communication style. This will give you insight into *yourself.* Understanding yourself better is the first step to understanding others.

Following is a quick and simple overview of the four personality styles from the perspective of dates.

Have you ever dated a guy who was all about *fun?* This guy is a social butterfly who's the life of the party and born to work a room. He's an extrovert, enjoys socializing, and likes to flirt. He's also a great storyteller. He doesn't like to be left out, and his calendar is full of social events. He dresses in colorful clothing and might own a fast or flashy car. With all of that activity, however, he can't always be relied on to get things done.

You might have a hard time getting this guy to commit. He's easily infatuated and may be seeking a casual one-night stand.

This guy is a **peacock.** Although he's a lot of fun, he may not stay in one place or with one person very long.

Peacock slogan: *I just want to have fun.*

This type is quite detailed oriented and dependable, and he likes structure. He asks a lot of questions and he's analytical. He's organized and always has your dates planned out (e.g., reservation made for a specific time and restaurant). He's an introvert and a bit of a perfectionist, drives a rather conservative car or SUV, dresses on the conservative side, and shows up on time. Lucky for you, he prefers a monogamous relationship. This type is an *owl.*

Owl slogan: *Who, what, when, where, and why?*

This personality type is supportive and a great listener. He's easy going, let's you decide where to have dinner, and isn't very aggressive. He avoids conflict. He likes to hug and is loyal to people in his life. He's low key and avoids risky situations, and he enjoys a peaceful environment with no drama. Fairly emotional, he might shed a few tears during a romantic movie, and he appreciates family values. He's a romantic and may give you little meaningful gifts but nothing extravagant. A gentleman, he opens the car door for you, and he prefers a committed relationship and long-term dating. This guy is a ***dove.***

Dove slogan: *Peace and love*

This guy is bold and sometimes blunt in his approach. He's impatient, likes to be in control, and asks for what he wants. He has a strong personality, is confident and highly decisive, likes challenges, and is quick to take action. He often has a title such as CEO, president, or entrepreneur. When he walks into a room, he owns the room and people notice him. Here we have an *eagle.*

Eagle slogan: *Just do it!*

Do you see how these four personality types are completely different?

Which personality type do you think you are?

Yes, you could be all four, but typically you have a combination of two primary types, a dominant and a secondary one.

I am a Dove/Owl, and my husband Tod is an Eagle/Peacock. Complete opposites. By knowing each other's personality style, we're able to understand each other more deeply. We understand why we each want certain things and why we act the way we act. While we don't always agree, we know why, which saves frustration and gives us more patience and grace.

As a Dove/Owl, I am reserved, private, and an introvert. I don't like a lot of people knowing my business. I'm a people pleaser. I like to get along with everyone and try to keep the peace. I don't like to think of myself as a homebody, but I do enjoy staying at home more often than going to social events. I prefer a quiet atmosphere. I dress conservatively and love comfortable clothes such as jeans, T-shirts, and yoga pants. I rarely splurge, love a good sale, and can spend an hour in Home Goods browsing the aisles.

As an Eagle/Peacock, my husband is very transparent and usually tells it like it is. He's blunt and doesn't hold back if he feels it will help someone be better or grow. A highly social guy, he can strike up a conversation with just about anyone. Tod is also confident. When he walks into a room, people notice him. He loves and thrives in social environments and at events. He likes to dress sharply in suits and colorful clothing. When he listens to music, he turns up the volume, and he likes to drive fast.

You can see we're very different, but despite that, we appreciate each other's qualities. Yes, certain qualities can annoy us, but we balance each other out.

Knowing what we each like and how we think helps us to bend a little to accommodate each other. We have a give-and-take relationship, which is essential for mutual satisfaction and happiness. It's not always easy; sometimes it takes intention, effort, sacrifice, and patience—but it's worth it!

I heard someone say once that a relationship is not 50/50; it's 100/100!

I hope this explanation of personality types has opened your eyes as to why you may clash with some people. These differences can cause multiple problems and even break up relationships. However, when opposites attract, it can be a great relationship if you understand each other. If you don't, your relationship could be complicated and unbalanced. Awareness will serve you well.

Now, are you ready for the story of how I met Tod? My love story is coming right up in Chapter 12!

Chapter 12

MY LOVE STORY

Being single doesn't mean no one wants you.
It just means God is busy writing your love story.
~ Anonymous

eople often ask me, "How did you and your husband meet?" I love to answer this question because the way Tod and I met is a fun, motivating, and life-changing story with lessons to share. Getting asked that question so often is *one* of the reasons that inspired me to write this book. At the end of the chapter, I'll explain how my experience may help *you* achieve your dream partner.

Meeting Tod has been life changing for me in four major ways, which I'll explain in no particular order of importance.

First, I probably would have never taken the leap to become an entrepreneur if it hadn't been for my husband. Before I met Tod, I never even entertained the idea, probably because of my personality type (not liking risk). Tod, however, is a natural entrepreneur, and working with him to run a business has stretched me in many areas of my life, both personally and professionally.

Second, Tod has helped strengthen my relationship with God. Now I continuously learn more about God's Word, which has changed the way I live my life. I enjoy less stress and more peace.

Third, I'm a better communicator. For decades, Tod has been teaching individuals and companies how to communicate more effectively. I've learned that open and honest communication is a must in my life and key to all healthy relationships.

Fourth, I'm now married to my best friend, business partner, and biggest cheerleader!

Let's look at how it all came about.

How I Met My Husband

During my single years, I worked as a licensed esthetician in Newport Beach, California. I love skincare, beauty products, and helping others with their skin care goals. However, I wasn't making enough income to support living in that area. I decided it was the perfect time in my life to focus on finding a new career. I started searching job sites online and submitted my résumé for every opportunity that looked like something I would enjoy and offered the salary I needed.

One beautiful sunny day, I received notice from one of the companies that strongly piqued my interest. Woohoo! I was chosen for an interview!

The position I'd applied for was a patient care coordinator at a plastic surgeon's office in Newport Beach, just minutes from where I lived. A patient care coordinator educates patients on the various surgeries, procedures, and products offered and closes the sale.

The interview for this position would be with Mr. Tod Novak and would take place via Skype (Zoom didn't exist at this time). I'd never had an interview over video conference and had never used Skype. This was twelve years ago, which was a much different time in the world of technology. I was *determined* to figure it out because the job sounded great, and I wasn't going to miss the opportunity to interview for it.

Tod Novak lived in Albuquerque, New Mexico. His company, The Novak Group, consulted with this plastic surgeon's office on improving office procedures and processes and sales techniques to increase booked procedures.

For the video interview, I would need to use a computer with a camera. I didn't have a camera on my computer at the time, and I wasn't especially tech savvy. Luckily, my girlfriend Tricia offered me her computer equipped with a camera, and she was familiar with Skype. She helped set me up for the interview without technical drama. Thank you, Tricia! The last thing I wanted was technical issues, which can happen easily, tech savvy or not.

I was nervous about the interview because I didn't have a lot of sales experience, and this job sounded out of my league. However, I had experience in the esthetic industry, and I was eager and willing to learn more about sales and whatever it would take to land the job.

Overall, the interview went well, considering how nervous I was. During the interview, I could feel my body heating up, and I was afraid I'd be bright red from head to toe. That happens when I'm nervous, but over the years, I've learned to control getting so nervous and looking like a red hot.

After the interview, I told Tricia I was quite interested in the job, and I also said, "You know, there's something about Tod Novak. I think I felt an attraction."

A few days went by; then I got an email with the news that I'd been selected for another interview. This one would be in person at the plastic surgeon's office. The interview was with the doctor and Tod Novak. They requested that I prepare a business plan and bring it to the interview. *What?!* I'd never put together a business plan and didn't even know where to begin. I immediately did my research and reached out to a few trusted friends for advice, and I managed to put together a business plan. I also went shopping for the perfect outfit for the interview to help me feel a little more confident.

When I arrived for the interview, I first met with Tod Novak because the doctor was busy with a patient consultation. It turned out his consultation took over an hour, so Tod and I sat in an office and visited. Our conversation was a little bit about the position but largely about other random topics.

Remember that attraction I felt during the Skype interview? Oh yeah, it was real! I was attracted even more after that hour-long one-on-one conversation.

The doctor finally joined us, and when we finished the interview, I was told they would make a final decision within the next few days. After I got home, I immediately sent a thank you email to both the doctor and Tod.

The following day was Friday and I didn't hear back from Tod. On Saturday, I was having brunch with my girlfriends, and my interview came up in conversation. They were anxious to hear details. I told them I'd probably find out on Monday if I got the job. I also shared that, after some thought, I decided if I didn't get the job I'd ask Tod if he'd like to meet for coffee or have dinner the next time he was in the area. I knew he visited Newport Beach at least once a month to work with the doctor's office. *However,* if I got the job, I wasn't going to mix business with pleasure. I'd keep my attraction hidden. My girlfriends agreed that sounded like a good strategy.

Then, during brunch, my cell phone rang. I glanced down and saw that Tod was calling me! I quickly excused myself from the table, stepped outside the restaurant, and took the call.

Tod said he was sorry to inform me I didn't get the job. As we were getting ready to end the call, I worked up the courage and said, "Well, this is kind of random, but next time you're in Newport Beach, would you be interested in meeting for coffee or dinner?"

Tod rather quickly ended the call and said he would get back to me. That was *not* the answer I was hoping for, and I didn't get a very good vibe from his response. I immediately figured he wasn't interested and wondered why in the world I'd put myself out there like that. I got a double rejection—no job and no date! *Ouch!*

When I joined the girls back at the table, they were anxious to hear how the call went. I proceeded to tell them the unfortunate news times two.

After brunch, when I was driving home, Tod called again. I thought maybe he had pocket dialed me by accident. I answered and he apologized for cutting me off so quickly earlier. He'd gotten a return call he was waiting for from a client. He went on to say he'd love to get together and would be back in Newport Beach in a few weeks. He asked if I would like to have dinner.

Even though I didn't get the job, I was a very happy girl. I had a dinner date scheduled with Tod Novak!

That was the beginning of our love story. From that day on, we spent two to three hours every night talking with each other on the phone. During those phone calls, I felt as if we got to know each other and connected well. We built a strong friendship and had deep conversations. I believe Tod

     Single KNOW More

and I learned more about each other in a few months than I learned about other guys I'd dated for a year or longer.

Six months into our long-distance relationship, Tod moved to Newport Beach, and we've literally been inseparable ever since.

My story got better with a little twist. The girl they hired as patient care coordinator at the plastic surgeon's office didn't work out, and I ended up getting the job! So in the end, I got the guy *and* the job! *SCORE!!*

I worked at the plastic surgery practice for about a year and then began my entrepreneurial journey with Tod and The Novak Group. This was definitely a mindset and lifestyle change, and it involved a huge leap of faith for me.

Certainly not all couples can work together, but it's been great for us. Tod and I enjoy spending time with each other. We're best friends, we communicate well, and we push each other and help each other grow personally and professionally. We have mutual big dreams and goals.

We have days when we need our respective personal space and we take it, but those days are rare. I think the reason I get asked so often how we met is because we spend so much time together and have such a close, loving relationship. That blows a lot of people away.

Tod and I continually work on our relationship and we *grow* together. I have matured as an individual, a wife, and a business owner. Just like everything in life, the more time and effort you put in, the better the outcome. Think about all the time and effort couples put into dating and planning their wedding. Then after they're married, often the planning and efforts just fade away.

Remember: *Grass is greener where you water it.*

Being in a long-term relationship isn't a ticket to being lazy. Don't ever take your relationship for granted and stop appreciating, giving, and caring. Yes, after a certain amount of time the excitement cools down, and that's normal. But you have to continually work on keeping the relationship alive and growing or it will stagnate or fizzle out!

Tod and I focus daily on small habits that support our relationship, such as giving each other a kiss almost every time we get out of the car. We also kiss each other every night before going to bed, and every morning we give each other a hug. Almost daily we say I love you. Some days Tod will tell me he loves me several times. It's those small daily habits that keep our bond strong.

I appreciate that Tod gets up in the morning before I do, grinds coffee beans, and makes pour-over coffee for the two of us. If you've ever made pour-over coffee, you know it's time consuming, but the fresh taste is worth the effort. I typically get up when I smell the coffee brewing. I give Tod a hug and thank him for the delicious cup of coffee that's waiting for me. Don't take simple love gestures for granted.

Change your habits and you change your life.

Tod is my biggest cheerleader. He believes I'm capable of doing anything, and sometimes more than I think I'm capable of doing. I feel super blessed to have a husband who believes in me so much.

I am proof that you can meet your dream guy anywhere when you're least expecting it. Through my single season, I never lost faith in love and I kept my heart open. I believe our meeting just fell into place in God's perfect timing.

Remember . . .

First work on building a solid foundation. This means loving and respecting yourself and becoming strong, confident, and grounded! The more you love and respect yourself, the better chance you have of attracting a man who also loves and respects you.

As you date, maintain high standards and values. Focus on what you want, not what you don't want. Every person you date has something to teach you, so learn from your experiences and keep your heart open.

You may experience times when you just want to work on yourself, such as learning new skills, developing your spirituality, or growing professionally. At these times, you may not care if you date or not—and that's fine. You don't want to be desperate about finding someone. When you're ready, get out there and open yourself up! Pay more attention to your surroundings than your phone. Take off your blinders and take an interest in people, live in the moment, and enjoy life. You may well find that your dream guy appears when you're least expecting it, just as mine did. Relax, trust, and be open to divine timing.

I hope this book has inspired and motivated you to always work on your foundation and that you share your inspirations with others who may also benefit.

You, my friend, are capable and worthy of an amazing life!

I wish you much love and success!

What brings me JOY!

- ♥ God
- ♥ My husband (Tod)
- ♥ Family
- ♥ Friends
- ♥ Helping others
- ♥ PJ's & slippers
- ♥ Comfy sweatshirts/yoga pants
- ♥ Face masks – (the kind that wash off)
- ♥ Exfoliating (head to toe)
- ♥ Glowing skin
- ♥ Coffee (my husband makes the best!)
- ♥ Organization
- ♥ Skin care/beauty products
- ♥ Beach
- ♥ Children's laughter
- ♥ Smiles
- ♥ Hair appointments
- ♥ My wedding ring
- ♥ Cozy fires
- ♥ Looking through old photos
- ♥ Flowers
- ♥ Massages
- ♥ Pedicures
- ♥ Pretty/feminine things
- ♥ Soft blankets

- ♥ Freedom
- ♥ Fall (my favorite season)
- ♥ Christmas and what it represents
- ♥ Nature
- ♥ Tacos/Guacamole
- ♥ Tod's famous Caesar salad
- ♥ Wedding Cake

What brings You JOY?!

Your turn …

____

____

____

____

____

____

____

____

Read your JOY list daily as a reminder of what you need to be incorporating into your life!

You deserve it! ♥

About the Author

Joyce Novak is vice president of The Novak Group, a full-service sales agency specializing in sales management, training, coaching, and communication. The love of her life, her husband Tod Novak, is the company's CEO. Joyce and Tod reside in Scottsdale, Arizona, and Newport Beach, California.

Start Building YOUR Healthy Solid Foundation!

Now that you have read *Single KNOW More* and are feeling inspired to start working on your foundation, you might be wondering, *"Where do I start?"*

1:1 personal coaching with Joyce!

Joyce is extending an opportunity for a select few to be personally coached by her. These sessions are tailored to address your unique needs and pave the way to help YOU build a healthy solid foundation and attract relationships you deserve!

To learn more details about 1:1 coaching:
Email: Joyce@singleknowmore.com
Subject Line: 1:1 Coaching with Joyce
Body of Email: Your full name and phone number.

If you enjoyed *Single KNOW More*, please pass the love on and send a copy to your single friends, family members, or anyone looking to improve their foundation.

Endnotes

1   Kara Cutruzzula, "Challenge Your Negative Thinking With the 5:1 Ratio," September 25, 2019. *https://advice.theshineapp.com/articles/challenge-your-negative-thinking-with-the-5-1-ratio/*. Last accessed June 22, 2022.

2   WebMD, Medically Reviewed by Dan Brennan, MD, "How Music Affects Mental Health," November 01, 2021. *https://www.webmd.com/mental-health/how-music-affects-mental-health/*. Last accessed June 23, 2022.

3   Centers for Disease Control and Prevention (CDC). "Fast Facts: Preventing Intimate Partner Violence." *https://www.cdc.gov/violenceprevention/intimatepartnerviolence/fastfact.html#*: See also: *https://www.safehorizon.org/get-informed/domestic-violence-statistics-facts/#definition/*. Both last accessed June 23, 2022.

4   Skin Cancer Foundation, "UV Radiation & Your Skin." *https://www.skincancer.org/risk-factors/uv-radiation/*. Last accessed June 23, 2022.

5   Brittny Reynolds, "Flowers Can Have a Positive Impact on Mental Health," Team Flower, n.d. *https://education.teamflower.org/learn/design/flowers-and-mental-health*. Last accessed June 22, 2022.
    See also: Tommy Williamson, "The Power of Beautiful Flowers and Their Impact on Mental Health," Positive Psychology, November 1, 2020. *https://www.psychreg.org/flowers-mental-health/*. Both last accessed June 23, 2022.

6   U. S. Department of Health & Human Services, National Heart, Lung, and Blood Institute, "What Are Sleep Deprivation and Deficiency?" n.d. *https://www.nhlbi.nih.gov/health/sleep-deprivation*. Last accessed June 23, 2022.

7   "American Heart Association Recommendations for Physical Activity in Adults and Kids." Last reviewed April. 18, 2018. *https://www.heart.org/en/healthy-living/fitness/fitness-basics/aha-recs-for-physical-activity-in-adults.* Last accessed June 23, 2022.

8   Well+Good, Rachel Lapidos, "Why Walking After Eating May be the Best Time to Get Those 10,000 Steps," updated March 14, 2022. *https://www.wellandgood.com/walking-after-eating/.* Last accessed June 23, 2022.

9   Harvard School of Public Health, T. H. Chan, "The Importance of Hydration," 2017. *https://www.hsph.harvard.edu/news/hsph-in-the-news/the-importance-of-hydration/. Last accessed June 23, 2022.*

10 Lifehack, Krissy Brady, "11 Benefits of Drinking Lemon Water (And How to Drink It for Good Health)," n.d. *https://www.lifehack.org/articles/lifestyle/11-benefits-lemon-water-you-didnt-know-about.html.* Last accessed June 25, 2022.

11 Madhuleena Roy Chowdhury, "The Neuroscience of Gratitude and How It Affects Anxiety & Grief," *PositivePsychology.com,* Grief & Bereavement, April 9, 2019. *https://positivepsychology.com/neuroscience-of-gratitude/.* Last accessed June 25, 2022.

12 Johns Hopkins Medicine, "5 Vaping Facts You Need to Know," reviewed by Michael Joseph Blaha, M.D., M.P.H., n.d. *https://www.hopkinsmedicine.org/health/wellness-and-prevention/5-truths-you-need-to-know-about-vaping.* See also: Centers for Disease Control and Prevention (CDC), Smoking and Tobacco Use, "Quick Facts on the Risks of E-cigarettes for Kids, Teens, and Young Adults," n.d. *https://www.cdc.gov/tobacco/basic_information/e-cigarettes/.* Both last accessed June 25, 2022.

13 Amber Brooks, "34 Interesting & Surprising Online Dating Statistics in 2022," *DatingAdvice.com, n.d. https://www.datingadvice.com/studies/iasods.* Last accessed June 25, 2022.

[14] Nicole Spector, "Smiling can trick your brain into happiness –
and boost your health," NBC NEWS, BETTER by TODAY,
updated January 9, 2018. *https://www.nbcnews.com/better/
health/smiling-can-trick-your-brain-happiness-boost-your-
health-ncna822591*. Last accessed June 28, 2022.

[15] Quora.com. https://www.quora.com/How-many-times-is-fear-
mentioned-in-the-Bible, n.d. Last accessed June 28, 2022.

[16] Certified Professional Career Coach, n.d. *https://cpcc-career-
coach.com/career-coaching-communicating-effectively-active-
listening/*. Last accessed June 28, 2022.

[17] John Brandon, "These Updated Stats About How Often You
Use Your Phone Will Humble You," Inc.com, n.d. *https://www.
inc.com/john-brandon/these-updated-stats-about-how-often-
we-use-our-phones-will-humble-you.html*. Last accessed
June 28, 2022.